Septuagint:

Tobit

Septuagint, Volume 11

SCRIPTURAL RESEARCH INSTITUTE
Published by Digital Ink Productions, 2024

Copyright

While every precaution has been taken in the preparation of this book, the publisher assumes no responsibility for errors or omissions, or for damages resulting from the use of the information contained herein.

Septuagint: Tobit

Second edition. March 5, 2024

Copyright © 2024 Scriptural Research Institute.

ISBN: 978-1-998288-56-4

The Septuagint was translated into Greek at the Library of Alexandria between 250 and 132 BC.

These English translations were created by the Scriptural Research Institute in 2019 through 2024, primarily from the Codex Vaticanus and Codex Sinaiticus, although many other Septuagint and Vetus Latina codices were also used for reference. Additionally the Oxyrhynchus Papyri 1076 and 1584 were used for comparative analysis.

The image used for the cover is 'Tobias Meets the Archangel Raphael' by Andrea Vaccaro, painted in 1583. The original painting is currently on display in the Museu Nacional d'Art de Catalunya, in Barcelona.

Table of Contents

TABLE OF CONTENTS

TABLE OF CONTENTS

Forward

In the mid 3rd century BC, King Ptolemy II Philadelphus of Egypt ordered a translation of the ancient Hebrew scriptures for the Library of Alexandria, which resulted in the creation of the Septuagint. The original version, published circa 250 BC, only included the Torah, or in Greek terms, the Pentateuch. The Torah is the five books traditionally credited to Moses, circa 1500 BC: Cosmic Genesis, Exodus, Leviticus, Numbers, and Deuteronomy. According to Jewish tradition, the original Torah was lost when the Babylonians destroyed the Temple of Solomon and was later rewritten by Ezra the Scribe from memory during the Second Temple period.

It is generally accepted that there were several versions of the ancient Aramaic and Phoenician scriptures before the translation of the Septuagint, although the older sections of the Torah appear to have originated in Akkadian Cuneiform. The version of the book of Tobit found in the Codex Vaticanus and most surviving copies of the Septuagint, was translated into Greek from Aramaic and added to the Septuagint, likely before 200 BC when the Judean Revolt against the Ptolemys rule, resulted in most Jews and Samaritans fleeing from Egypt, either east into Judea, or south into Nubia. There is another version of the Book of Tobit found in the Codex Sinaiticus, which appears to be older than the version in the other codices, and not translated in the

Ptolemy's Egypt, but somewhere in the Seleucid's Empire.

The Book of Tobit appears to be from an older sect of Judaism, likely the one led by the 'false priest' Tobiah, who was expelled from the temple by Ezra when his genealogy could not be proven in 2nd Ezra. 2nd Ezra was the version of Ezra used by the Pharisee sect which emerged under the Hasmonean Dynasty, while Tobit, along with Enoch, Jubilees, and Job appears to have primarily been used by the Essenes sects.

The Book of Tobit is generally viewed as fiction by most scholars for a variety of reasons. One major reason it is viewed as fiction is the presence of Tobit's cousin Ahikar, in both versions of the book, who is the protagonist of the Words of Ahikar, a book set in the same era, which is also considered fiction. It is quite clear from the text of Tobit, that it is the same Ahikar, and not just someone with the same name, as Ahikar's betrayal by his nephew is mentioned, which is part of the early section of Ahikar. Nevertheless, both books, Tobit and Ahikar survive in various forms, meaning that they were edited multiple times before the versions that survive to the present were transcribed.

The surviving copies of the Septuagint include two versions of the Book of Tobit, the more common form, found in the Codex Vaticanus, Codex Alexandrinus, and most other surviving copies of the Septuagint, and the less common version found in the Codex Sinaiticus. Additionally, fragments of Tobit found among the Oxyrhynchus Papyri don't match either the Vaticanus or Sinaiticus version of Tobit. The Oxyrhynchus Papyri are a collection of ancient texts found in southern Egypt dating to the Greek, Roman, and Byzantine eras of Egyptian history, approximately 300 BC to 640 AD. Among the Oxyrhynchus Papyri, two fragments of Tobit have been found, Papyrus 1594, dated to circa 275 AD, and Papyrus 1076, dated to circa 550 AD. Unfortunately, these fragments are extremely short, with only a few lines surviving from chapters 12 and 2 respectively. The Oxyrhynchus Papyri fragments of Tobit are in Greek but do not match surviving versions found in the Septuagint codices, meaning there were no less than three Greek versions of Tobit in circulation by 350 AD, when the Codex Vaticanus and Codex Sinaiticus are dated to.

While the Greek translations must have originated in an Aramaic text, it does not survive to the present. Nor have any Hebrew translations been found, and it is possible it was not translated into Hebrew, as the text is contrary to the theology of Simon the Zealot, who originally ordered the creation of the Hebrew translations of the ancient Israelite scriptures. The Peshitta does include a version of Tobit that may have been translated directly from the Aramaic source, however, western scholarship leans towards it having been translated from the Septuagint.

The differences between the Vaticanus and Sinaiticus versions of Tobit are too extensive to treat the books as the same book, however, their story is essentially the same. The two books must have had a common source, however, the Sinaiticus's version is over 20% longer than the Vaticanus's version, and appears to be an older version of Tobit. One of the reasons that the Book of Tobit is interpreted as fiction, is the existence of historical errors and anachronisms found in the Vaticanus version, which includes the Babylonian king Nebuchadnezzar (Ναβουχοδονοσορ) and the Persian king Xerxes (Ασυηρος) jointly destroying Nineveh, the capital of the Assyrian Empire. Nineveh was sacked by Babylonian King Nabopolassar in 612 BC, along with Median and Persian allies, led by the Median King Cyaxares, who then integrated the city into his Median Empire. Nabopolassar's son Nebuchadnezzar, who assumed the throne in 605 BC, finally conquered the remnants of the Assyrian forces in Syria at the Battle of Carchemish that same year, however, he did not attack or destroy Nineveh. Meanwhile, the name Ahasuerus (Ασυηρος) was the Aramaic name of Xerxes, the Persian king who ruled between 486 and 465 BC.

These anachronisms are not found in the Codex Sinaiticus' version, which does not mention either king, but gives credit to King Achiacharos (Αχιαχαρος) of Media, which is likely an attempt to transliterate the Median name of King Cyaxares into Aramaic. Cyaxares's Median name was Uvaxshtra (𒀭-𒈗), however, it was transliterated several ways into the languages and scripts of the day, including the Babylonian Úaksatar (𒌑𒀝𒊓𒋻), the Elamite Makiišturri (𒈠𒆠𒅖𒌇𒊑), the Phrygian Ksuwaksaros (ΚϹΟΛΑΥϹΡΟϹ), and the Greek Cyaxares (Κυαξάρης) from which the modern English name is derived.

The Sinaiticus version of Tobit describes King Achiacharos as conquering Nineveh and integrating it into his Median Kingdom, which, was done by King Cyaxares according to the Median, Persian, Babylonian, Egyptian, and Greek records from the era, and so, even if the origin of the name is disputed, the person described is King Cyaxares. There are several differences between the Vaticanus and Sinaiticus versions that point to the Sinaiticus version being older, and that point to the Vaticanus version being a later translation created in Alexandria, likely from an Aramaic early-Jewish redaction of the original Aramaic version.

Tobit's book was largely about his son Tobiah's journey to Ecbatana, the capital of the kingdom of Media, in the territory of northern modern Iran. The journey is set circa 673 BC, during the reign of King Esarhaddon of Assyria. After inheriting the Assyrian throne in 681 BC, when two of his brothers had killed his father Sennacherib, Esarhaddon spent several years suppressing rebellions across his empire, that some historians believe were in support of his older brother Arda-Mulissu, who had led the conspiracy to kill their father, and then fled to Urartu after a six-week civil war against Esarhaddon for the throne. These campaigns across the empire led to additional campaigns into the Caucasus Mountains, Anatolia, and the Arabian Peninsula, as well as Media, where several tribes of Medes were subjugated into the empire. Esarhaddon's conquests culminated in the conquest of Egypt in 671 BC, however, he could not capture Kush itself, which had been ruling Egypt for centuries by the time the Assyrians captured it.

It is unclear how much control thee Assyrians exercised over Media, as several tribes of Medes did agree to pay tribute after the Assyrians defeated the Median chiefs Eparna and Shidirparna circa 675 BC, however, a chief the Assyrians called Kashtariti (𒅖𒐊𒈪𒀖𒄿𒀖), which the Old Persian records later transliterated as Xšaθrita (𒀴𒐊𒍝𒅗𒐊𒋾𒈾) continued to attack the Assyrians throughout Esarhaddon's reign. It has been theorized that this was the legendary King Phraortes (𒀭𒁹𒆷𒊑𒀀𒊭), which according to Old Persian records, started a war against the Assyrians, and was ultimately killed by Esarhaddon's heir Ashurbanipal. It is also possible that he was one of many Median chiefs that did not recognize the authority of the Assyrians, as the surviving records indicated the region swung rapidly back and forth between Assyrian control and Median rebellion.

Tobiah's traveling companion to Ecbatana was the angel Raphael, who disguised himself as a Naphtalite to help Tobiah marry his cousin, who was possessed by an ancient Zoroastrian demon. After returning from Ecbatana, Raphael healed Tobit, who had lost his sight eight years earlier. The story continues after Tobit died, with Tobiah moving to Ecbatana, which implies he continued writing his father's book. It is unclear how or when the book was carried from Media to Judea and Egypt, however, this likely happened during the Persian era, when all the lands were under the same empire.

In 200 BC, the Greek Kingdom of Syria under the Seleucid Dynasty took Judea from Egypt, and began an effort to Hellenize the Judeans, which effectively banned traditional Judaism. This Hellenizing activity was partially successful, creating the Sadducee faction of

Judaism, however, it also led to the Maccabean Revolt in 165 BC, which itself created the independent Kingdom of Judea. This Kingdom had a tenuous alliance with the Roman Republic until General Pompey conquered Syria into the Roman Republic in 69 BC. Pompey's goal was to liberate Greek-speaking communities in the Middle East that had fallen under the rule of non-Greeks when the Seleucids Syrian Empire had collapsed, and he carved up Judea, and Edom to the east, placing Greek-speaking cities under the protection of the Roman province of Syria. He also liberated several smaller communities that had been occupied by Judea, granting them self-government, including Ashdod, Yavne, Jaffa, Dora, Marissa, and Samaria.

A series of wars including both Julius Caesar's campaigns, and a Parthian invasion led to the weakening of the Hasmonean dynasty, and in 37 AD, the Roman Senate appointed Herod the Great as King of the Jews. Herod's rule wasn't particularly popular, as he allowed the Romans to establish themselves within Judea, however, he did expand Judea, reintegrating the Greek and Samaritan cities, and annexing Galilee and Edom. When he died, his kingdom was divided between four successors, a situation that ended in 66 AD when the Romans conquered the region. An uprising in 120 AD led to the Jews being exiled from Judea, and the region became a Greco-Roman colony. In the wake of the Jews, the Samaritans rose in numbers, along with the Christians once Christianity was legalized. Between 529 and 555 AD, the Samaritans revolted and were effectively annihilated, by Constantinople the Eastern Roman capital.

Outside of Judea, the Septuagint was the dominant form of Jewish scriptures across the Greek-speaking world, which by the beginning of the Christian era extended from the Roman Empire in the west, to the Indo-Greek Kingdom in the east. Jewish traders had established small colonies along the trade routes of the Red Sea and the Indian Ocean, reaching as far south as Yemen, and as far east as southern India, and these Jews spoke Greek and used the Septuagint.

The earliest Christian Bibles, all used the Septuagint, however, by the 4th century some Christian scholars were debating whether they should retranslate the Old Testament from the version the Jews were using, and some even suggested using the Samaritan version. Both suggestions were generally dismissed as heretical, as Jesus and the Apostles had quoted from the Septuagint, even though they had access to the Hebrew version then in use. This argument held in the west until the Middle Ages, when Catholic Bibles switched to the Masoretic Texts. In the east, Orthodox Bibles continued to use the

Septuagint, as they do today. To the south, the Ethiopian Tewahedo Church continued to use the Septuagint, and across Asia, the Thomas Christians and Nestorians continued to use the Septuagint. Only in Western Europe were the later Masoretic Text adopted, abandoning the more ancient Septuagint, on the assumption that the Jews had copied their texts more faithfully than the Greeks had translated them. This assumption carried forward into the Protestant Churches that broke off from the Catholic Church, and therefore almost all Protestant Bibles use the Masoretic Texts for the basis of the Old Testament.

Unfortunately, this means that the earliest Christian writing is generally confusing and ignored by Protestants and Catholics. The earliest Christians of the first and second ages quoted books that are no longer in the Bible, and as such, their writings are not always understood. Septuagint: Tobit is a 21st century translation aimed at correcting this problem. As the Pharisees did not use Tobit, the Masoretes did not copy it, and therefore it is not found in the Masoretic Text. When the Catholics and Protestants switched from the Septuagint to the Masoretic Texts as the basis of the Old Testament, the book of Tobit was relegated to the Apocrypha in Catholic Bibles, and then later generally dropped from Protestant bibles.

FORWARD

One of the problems with academic translations of the Septuagint, is the use of unfamiliar names or terms, as the Septuagint was in Greek, and therefore many names are unrecognizable to modern English readers who are used to Hebrew-derived names. This project uses the more commonly understood Hebrew-derived names instead of their Greek translations, such as Canaan instead of Chanaan, and Melchizedek instead of Melchisedec. Common modern names are also used instead of either Greek or Hebrew terms when geographical locations are known, such as the archaeological name Uruk instead of the Greek Orech, or the Hebrew Erech, and the archaeological term Sumer instead of Shinar or Senar. While this could be argued as not being a correct academic procedure, it does fulfill the goal of making the translation easy to read and understand.

Tobit (Vaticanus): Chapter 1

The book of the words of Tobit,[1] son of Tobiel, son of Ananiel, son of Aduel, son of Gabael of the descendants of Asahel, of the tribe of Naphtali, who in the time of King Sargon II[2] of the Assyrians was led captive out of Tishbe,[3] which is to the right of Kadesh of Naphtali in Galilee near Asher.

I, Tobit, have followed all the days of my life in the ways of truth and justice, and I was very charitable to my brothers from my nation, who came with me to Nineveh in the land of the Assyrians. When I was still young in my own country of Israel, all of my father's tribe of Naphtali abandoned the temple in Jerusalem,[4] which was chosen out of all the tribes of Israel that all the tribes should sacrifice there, where the temple and tabernacle[5] of the Highest[6] was consecrated and built for all ages.

All the tribes which joined together sacrificed to Ba'al the calf,[7] including the house of Naphtali my father Naphtali.

I regularly went by myself to Jerusalem at the feasts, as it was ordained to all Israel by an eternal decree, having the tithe of the animals and the first-born, with that which was first cut, and I gave them to the priests, the sons of Aaron, the firstborns for the altar, and the tithe I gave to the Levites who served in Jerusalem. A second tenth I would spend on everything in Jerusalem, each year. The third amount I gave as it was my duty, as Debora my father's mother had commanded me, because I was left an orphan by my father.

When I had come to the age of a man, I married my relative Hannah, and through her, I became the father of Tobiah. When we were taken away captives to Nineveh, all my brothers and those that were of my families ate the food of the nations, but I kept myself from eating it because I remembered God with all my heart. The Highest gave me grace and favor before Sargon II, so that I became the purchaser of his provisions. I went into Media,[8] and once left in trust with Gabael, the brother of Gabri, in the Median city of Ray[9] ten talents of silver.

When Sargon II was dead, Sennacherib[10] his son reigned in his place, whose land was troubled and I could not go into Media. In the time of Sargon, I was very charitable to my brothers and gave my bread to the hungry, my clothes to the naked, and if I saw any of my nation dead, or thrown out of the walls of Nineveh, I buried him. If King Sennacherib killed any, when he came back from Judea, I buried them privately, for in his anger he killed many, but the bodies were not found when they were searched for by the king.

When one of the Ninevites went and complained about me to the king, that I buried them, I hid, knowing that I was being searched for, to be put to death, and I ran away in fear. Then, all my goods were seized and there was nothing left to me, other than my wife Hannah and my son Tobiah. Less than fifty days passed, before two of his sons killed him,[11] and they fled into the mountains of Urartu,[12] and Esarhaddon[13] his son reigned in his place, who appointed over his father's accounts, and over all his affairs, Ahikar[14] my brother Anael's son. Ahikar asked about me, and I returned to Nineveh. Ahikar was cup-bearer, and keeper of the signet, and steward, and overseer of the accounts, and Esarhaddon appointed him second to himself, and he was my nephew.

Tobit (Vaticanus): Chapter 1 Notes

1 Codex Vaticanus: Tôbit (ⲧⲱⲃⲉⲓⲧ)

• Codex Sinaiticus: Tôbith (ⲧⲱⲃⲉⲓⲑ)

• LXX 106: Tôbit (Ⲧⲟⲟⲩⲧ)

• LXX 248: Tôbêt (Ⲧⲟⲟⲩⲏⲧ)

• LXX 392: Tôbid (Ⲧⲟⲟⲩϭⲓⲁ)

The names in the various manuscripts of the book of Tobit/Tobith/Tobid are not standardized, including the names of the book itself. This indicates three or more separate translations into Greek, as no one would have a reason to change the names if redacting one to make the other. The more common English name 'Tobit' is used in this translation.

2 Codex Vaticanus: Enemessarou (ⲉⲛⲉⲙⲉⲥⲥⲁⲣⲟⲩ)

• LXX 46: Ennemesarou (Ⲉⲛⲛϭⲙϭⲥⲁⳡⲟⲩ)

• LXX 71: Enemesarou (Ⲉⲛϭⲙϭⲥⲁⳡⲟⲩ)

• LXX 318: Enaimesarou (Ⲉⲛⲁⲓⲙϭⲥⲁⳡⲟⲩ)

• Septuagint ms 122: Enemesarrou (Ⲉⲛϭⲙϭⲥⲁⳡⳡⲟⲩ)

• LXX 249: Enemassarou (Ⲉⲛϭⲙⲁⲥⲥⲁⳡⲟⲩ)

• LXX 107: Nemessarou (Ⲛϭⲙϭⲥⲥⲁⳡⲟⲩ)

• Sahidic manuscripts: Namessaros (Ⲛⲁⲙⲉⲥⲥⲁⲣⲟⲥ)

Based on the rest of the book this must be a reference to Sargon II, King of Assyria between 722 and 705 BC. The name is often mistranslated as Shalmaneser, however, Enemessarou's son is later identified as Sennacherib, who was Sargon II's son. Shalmaneser was recorded in the books of the Kingdoms (Masoretic Kings), as having conquered Samaria, however, while Shalmaneser V's armies did besiege Samaria for three years, he died before Samaria surrendered, and when they surrendered, it was to Sargon II, Shalmaneser V's heir, who recorded in his records that he deported 27,920 Samaritans to Assyria.

This appears to have been an Aramaic translation of his Assyrian name Šarru-kīnum (𒈗𒄀𒈾), with the Assyrian terms inverted to Kīnum-šarru. His name is believed to translate as approximately as 'king who is legitimate,' suggesting the Aramaic translator interpreted then name as 'legitimate king,' and was not basing the reference on a historic record of the king, after his throne name had become standardized, but lived in the era of Sargon II.

Assuming this is a reference to Sargon, which it appears to be, it is notable that in the Book of Isaiah, the name Šarru-kīnum is rendered as Sargôn (סַרְגוֹן), meaning that the Book of Tobit is not dependent on Isaiah, and was likely translated into Aramaic by someone who had not read Isaiah. This supports the author's claims to be a Samaritan living in Assyria, and the dating of the text to the era of the Assyrian

Empire. The Hebrew-derived name 'Sargon' is used in this translation, as it is more common in modern English.

3 Codex Vaticanus: Tishbes (ⲐⲓⲤⲂⲎⲤ)

- Codex Alexandrinus: Thêbês (ⲐⲎⲂⲎⲤ)

- Peshitta: Thbhš (ܬܒܒܫ). Translation: Thebes

- Codex Corbeiensis (VL 150): Bibel

- Codex Sangermanensis 4 (VL 7 : Viel

- Codex Complutensis 1 (VL 109): Biel

- Codex Monacensis (VL 130): Cibiel

- Codex Bobbiensis (VL 135): Sibiel

- Ge'ez ms.: Tebesi (ጠቤሲ). Translation: Thebes

The Vaticanus and Sinaiticus manuscripts agree that is was the accepted Greek translation of the town called Tishbe (תִּשְׁבֶּ) in Hebrew, however, not all biblical scholars agree that there was a town called Tishbe in the Masoretic Texts. The issue revolves around the meaning of the word tishbi (תִּשְׁבִּי), which could simply be interpreted as 'resident,' however, was traditionally interpreted as Tishbite, meaning someone from Tishbe. The prophet Elijah was recorded as being a Tishbite, or maybe a 'resident,' in the Masoretic Kings (3rd Kingdoms) chapter 17. The Septuagint's translation is clearer, where he is recorded as being a Tishbite from Tishbe (Θεσβίτης ἐκ Θεσβων), and so this translation accepts the traditional interpretation of the name Tishbe. It is significant though, that Elijah was closely connected with the Assyrian Samaritans on the Khabur River, where he saw the cherubs and the flying chariot in the cloud of fire and lightning. If he was from the same town as those relocated by Sargon II, it would make sense for him to visit them, as they would have been his cousins.

A large number of Greek, Latin, Syriac, and Ge'ez manuscripts deviate on this name, with the largest alternate reading being Thebes. It is unclear if this was intended to represent Thebes in Egypt, or Greece, or another town in the mind of the translator. Thebes was a city in Greece at the time, however, the city later renamed Thebes in Egypt, was still known as was still known as Wôst (𓏏).

The name Thêbês (ΘΗΒΗС) in the Codex Vaticanus, and Thebes (ΘΕΒΕС) in the Codex Alexandrinus, was also used as a translation for a name of a town in Canaan in the book of Judges chapter 9. The town's name is rendered as Tbs (תבץ) in the Aleppo Codex, and Tēbēs (תֵבֵץ) in the Leningrad Codex, and is generally accepted as being Tubas (طوباس) in the northern area of the modern Palestinian West Bank. As this is in the region where Tishbe (תִּשְׁבֶּ) was supposed to have been located, it is possible that both names refer to the same town.

4 Codex Vaticanus: oecou Ierosolymôn (ΟΙΚΟΥ ΙΕΡΟϹΟΛΥΜω). Translation: house (or temple) in Jerusalem

• Codex Sinaiticus: Ierousalêm poleôs (ΙΕΡΟΥϹΑΛΗΜ ΠΟΛΕωϹ). Translation: Jerusalem town

5 Codex Vaticanus: catascênôseôs (ΚΑΤΑϹΚΗΝωϹΕωϹ). Translation: camping place

This is most likely an attempt to translate 'tabernacle' into Greek via Aramaic, and so the more common term is used in this translation.

6 Codex Vaticanus: ypsístou (ΥΨΙϹΤΟΥ). Translation: highest

The Highest is a reference to God, or a god, found in many ancient religions in the region. According to the Torah, the ancient people of Salem worshiped El Elyon, which translates as Highest God when Abraham passed through the regions. The term Highest repeats through other early Jewish and Samaritan texts.

7 The codices tell essentially the same story, however, the Codex Vaticanus version appears to be a Jewish redaction of the Codex Sinaiticus version. The setting of the event is during the life of Jeroboam II, the king of Samaria between circa 768 and 746 BC. His kingdom briefly conquered the Arameans of Damascus and Hama, creating the largest

Israelite kingdom since the era of King David, and the largest that is known archaeologically, as evidence of the earlier United Kingdom of Israel has yet to be found. He was recorded as building shrines with icons of the calf-god in them, which outraged the prophets at the time, including Amos. The Vaticanus's reference to the Ba'al calf is anachronistic, as the god Ba'al Hadad was not depicted as a calf, although he was depicted as having horns, like many Middle-eastern gods. Based on the archaeological evidence, such as the potshards discovered at Khirbet el-Kom and Kuntillet Ajrud, the calf-god worshiped in Samaria circa 800 BC was Yahweh.

8 Codex Vaticanus: Midian (ⲘⲎⲆⲒⲀⲚ)

Media was the name of the land of the Medes, and ancient Iranian people who lived in northern Iran before the rise of the Persian Empire. The Medians were the allies of the Babylonians that jointly conquered the Assyrian Empire, a few decades after the story is set.

9 Codex Vaticanus: Ragoes (ⲢⲀⲄⲞⲒⳞ)

- LXX 318: Ragoê (Ρⲁγⲟⲏ)

- LXX 670: Raga (Ρⲁγⲁ)

- LXX 319: Rassois (ΡⲁⲥⲥⲟⲓⳞ)

- LXX 64: Agrois (ⲀγβⲟⲓⳞ)

This is accepted as the Greek name of Ray (ری), an ancient city near Tehran in Iran. It is regarded as the oldest continuously inhabited city in Tehran Province, dating back to the Median Empire. The Greek name used in this book is likely a transliteration of the Aramaic name from the era, itself transliterated from the Assyrian name Raga (𒀭𒆜𒐊𒆳𒁕). The older Elamite name was Rakkaan (𒁹𒅆𒀹), while the later Old Persian name was Ragae (𒐊𒋼𒐖𒐊).

10 Codex Vaticanus: Sennachirim (ⲥⲉⲛⲛⲁⲭⲏⲣⲓⲙ)

- Codex Venetus (LXX V): Chirim (ⲭⲉⲓⲣⲉⲓⲙ)

- LXX 74: Rim (ⲣⲓμ)

- LXX 314: Chirim (ⲭⲓρⲓμ)

- LXX 98: Senachrim (ⲥⲟ́ⲛⲁⲭρⲟ́ⲓμ)

- LXX 318: Senachirim (ⲥⲟ́ⲛⲁⲭⲟ́ⲓρⲟ́ⲓμ)

- LXX 106: Senachirim (ⲥⲟ́ⲛⲁⲭⲓρⲟ́ⲓμ)

- LXX 130: Senachrim (ⲥⲟ́ⲛⲁⲭρⲓμ)

- LXX 71: Senachirim (ⲥⲟ́ⲛⲁⲭⲟ́ⲓρⲓμ)

- LXX 76: Senachirim (ⲥⲟ́ⲛⲁⲭⲓρⲓμ)

- LXX 402: Senacherim (ⲥⲟ́ⲛⲁⲭⲟ́ρⲟ́ⲓμ)

- LXX 126: Senachechrim (ⲥⲟ́ⲛⲁⲭⲟ́ⲭρⲓμ)

- LXX 319: Senachri (ϲⲉ́ⲛⲁⲭⲣⲓ)

- LXX 46: Sennachrib (ϲⲉ́ⲛⲛⲁⲭⲣⲟ́ⲓⲱ)

- LXX 44: Naxim (ⲛⲁⲭⲓⲙ)

- Sahidic manuscripts: Senakherim (Ⲥⲉⲛⲁⲭⲉⲣⲓⲙ)

King Sennacherib was the king of the Assyrian Empire between 705 and 681 BC. His reign was spent fighting a series of insurrections in Babylonia and Canaan. He also launched a punitive invasion of Elam, that virtually wiped out the nation. His campaigns in Canaan included laying siege to Jerusalem, which had previously been allied to Assyria.

11 This was the year 681 BC, when Sennacherib was killed by his sons Arda-Mulissu and Nabu-shar-usur. This is calculated by Assyriologists as having taken place on 20 October, meaning Tobit would have gone into hiding sometime in early September.

12 Codex Vaticanus: Ararath (ⲁⲣⲁⲣⲁⲑ)

- Codex Sinaiticus: Ararat (ⲁⲣⲁⲣⲁⲧ)

- Sahidic manuscripts: Ararad (ⲁ̀ⲣⲁⲣⲁⲁ)

The Assyrian records record the princes as retreating to the Kingdom of ᵏᵘʳUrartu (𒆳𒌛𒆳) in the Armenian Highlands. The name of this country was recorded as Ararat (אֲרָרַט) in Hebrew, and Urartu (Ուրարտու) in Armenian. The Greek name is a transliteration of the Hebrew name, however, the more common historical name of Urartu is used in this translation.

13 Codex Vaticanus: Sacherdonos (ⲤⲀⲭⲈⲣⲆⲞⲚⲞⲤ)

* Codex Alexandrinus: Sacherdan (ⲤⲀⲭⲈⲣⲆⲀⲚ)

* Codex Venetus: Nacherdonos (ⲚⲀⲭⲈⲣⲆⲞⲚⲞⲤ)

* LXX 74: Sacherdônos (ⲤⲁⲭⲟⲣⲆⲱⲛⲟⲥ)

* LXX 314: Sacherdon (ⲤⲁⲭⲟⲣⲆⲟⲛ)

* LXX 538: Sacherdôn (ⲤⲁⲭⲟⲣⲆⲱⲛ)

* LXX 64: Sarchedonos (ⲤⲁⲣⲭⲟⲆⲟⲛⲟⲥ)

* LXX 46: Sachedôr (ⲤⲁⲭⲟⲆⲱⲣ)

* LXX 248: Acherdonos (ⲀⲭⲟⲣⲆⲟⲛⲟⲥ)

* LXX 98: Achirdônos (ⲀⲭⲟⲣⲆⲱⲛⲟⲥ)

* LXX 542: Nachordanos (ⲚⲁⲭⲟⲣⲆⲁⲆⲛⲟⲥ)

* Sahidic manuscripts: Sakherdônias (ⲤⲁⲭⲉⲣⲆⲱⲚⲓⲁⲥ)

* Armenian Bible: Asordan (Ասորդւաւ)

* Codex Corbeiensis (VL 150): Archedonassar

* Codex Monacensis (VL 130): Arcedonossar

* Codex Bobbiensis (VL 135): Nachoda

• Codex Complutensis 1 (VL 109): Natordan

Esarhaddon is the more common name of King Aššur-Aha-Iddina, Sennacherib's youngest son and heir. The name Esarhaddon is derived from the Latin Hazor Haddan, which was in turn derived from the Greek Asarchaddon (Ασαρχαδδων), which was used in direct translations from Assyrian texts. Sacherdonos (Σαχερδονος) appears to be a Greek transliteration of the Aramaic version of his name.

14 Codex Vaticanus: Achiacharon (ΑΧΙΑΧΑΡΟΝ)

• Codex Sinaiticus: Achicharon (ΑΧΙΧΑΡΟΝ)

• LXX 107: Achiachar (Αχιαχαρ)

• Vetus Latina manuscripts: Achicarum

This name is generally translated as Ahikar, the famous, possibly fictional hero of the Words of Ahikar, the oldest known Jewish or Samaritan text to survive intact to the present. The oldest copy found to date is from around 500 BC, a couple of centuries older than the oldest of the Dead Sea Scrolls. Tobit does allude to the story of Ahikar's betrayal by his nephew, which is found in the Words of Ahikar, and it is accepted that this was a reference to that Ahikar, however, both stories are also regarded as fiction by most scholars, and so the authors may have been the same person.

It is also possible that both books began as historical texts that then became fictionalized, however, if additional elements were added, they must have been added to the Words of

Ahikar before the oldest surviving copy, from circa 500 BC. As both Ahikar and Tobit are reported to have lived circa 700 BC, this is not a great deal of time for the books to have been altered, however, as all books were copied by hand at the time, it is possible that the scribes felt a more fantastic version of the tales of these two men's lives would sell better.

Tobit (Vaticanus): Chapter 2

When I returned home again, my wife Hannah was restored to me, along with my son Tobiah. At the feast of Pentecost, which is the holy feast of the seven weeks, there was a good dinner prepared for me, in which I sat down to eat. When I saw the abundance of food, I said to my son, "Go and bring whatever poor man you find from among our brothers, who worships the Lord,[1] and I'll wait for you."

But when he returned he said, "Father, one of our nation is strangled, and is throw out in the marketplace."

Then, before I had tasted any of the food, I got up and took him up into a room to wait until the sun went down. Then I returned, and washed myself, and ate my food in hunger, remembering the prophecy of Amos,[2] when he said, 'Your feasts will be turned into mourning, and all your happiness into sadness.' I wept, and after the sun set, I went and dug a grave and buried him.

My neighbors mocked me, and said, "This man is not afraid to be put to death over this matter, he who ran away. Look, he buries the dead again."

The same night I returned from the burial, I slept by the wall of my courtyard, as I was unclean. My face was uncovered, and I did not know that there were sparrows in the wall, and while my eyes were open, the sparrows dropped warm dung into my eyes. A white film came into my eyes, and I went to the physicians, but they could not help me. However, Ahikar took care of me, until he went to Elam.[3]

My wife Hannah took women's work. Once, when she had sent them home to the owners, they paid her wages and also gave her a goat. When it was in my house and began to bleat, I demanded of her, "Where did this goat come from? Is it stolen? Return it to the owners, for it is not lawful to eat anything that is stolen."

But she replied to me, "It was given as a gift in addition to my wages."

I did not believe her and commanded her to return it to its owners, and I was angry with her, but she replied to me, "Where are your charitable works and your righteous deeds? Look, are all your works known?"

Tobit (Vaticanus): Chapter 2 Notes

1 Codex Vaticanus: cyriou (ΚΥΡΙΟΥ). Translation: lord (or main, chief, dominant, master)

• LXX 249: Cyriô (Κυρίῳ). Translation: lord (or main, chief, dominant, master)

In some early fragments of the Septuagint, the name Iaw (Ιαω), Greek for Yahweh, survives instead of the term Lord (Κυρίου), however, there is no surviving text of Tobit that includes the name, and based on Tobit's referring to the Ba'al calf, it seems unlikely he worshiped Yahweh, or that the name would have been in his writing.

2 The Prophet Amos was active in Samaria and Judah between 760 and 755 BC, and is believed to have died in 745 BC, about 66 years before this event.

3 Codex Vaticanus: Ellymaeda (ΕΛΛΥΜΑΙΔΑ)

• Codex Sinaiticus: Elymaeda (ΕΛΥΜΑΙΔΑ)

• LXX 107: Elimaeda (ΕλιμΑΙΔΑ)

• LXX 98: Eloemaeda (ΕλοιμΑΙΔΑ)

• LXX 71: Elemaeda (ΕλϬμΑΙΔΑ)

• LXX 126: Lymaeda (ΛυμΑΙΔΑ)

• Codex Corbeiensis (VL 150): Limaidam

• Codex Monacensis (VL 130): Lymaidem

Haltamti (𒀸𒇆𒆠𒄿𒅎) was a major nation in southern modern Iran, until it was virtually destroyed by the kings of Assyria in the 7th century BC. The Babylonian name of the land was Elamma^{ki} (𒉏𒈣𒆠), which was adopted into Hebrew as Elam (עֵילָם) and Greek as Elám (Ελάμ), ultimately resulting in the modern English name Elam. The conflict in question is likely the events near the beginning of Esarhaddon's rule, when an ethnically Elamite Assyrian governor named Nabu-zer-kitti-lišir in southern Babylonia revolted against Assyrian rule and besieged Ur. Esarhaddon's army defeated Nabu-zer-kitti-lišir, and he fled to Elam, where he was ultimately captured and executed.

Tobit (Vaticanus): Chapter 3

I began to cry, and in my grief prayed, "Sydyk exists! Lord, all your works and all your ways are mercy and truth, and you judge truly and justly forever. Remember me! See me, but don't punish me for my sins and ignorance, and the sins of my fathers, who have sinned before you. They did not obey your commandments, and therefore you have given us as a plunder, and into captivity, and to death, and as an example of reproach to all the nations among whom we are dispersed. Now, your judgments are many and true. Deal with me according to my sins and my fore-fathers' because we have not kept your commandments, nor have walked honestly before you. Now, therefore, deal with me as seems best to you, and command my spirit to be taken from me, that I may be dissolved, and become dirt, for it is preferable for me to die rather than to live, because I have heard false insults, and have much sorrow. Command therefore that I may now be delivered out of this distress, and go into the everlasting place. Don't turn your face away from me."

The same day, in the Median city of Ecbatana,[1] Sarah the daughter of Raguel was also insulted by her father's woman-slaves because she had been married to seven husbands who Asmodeus[2] the evil spirit[3] had killed before they had lain with her.

"Do you not know," said they, "that you have strangled your husbands? You have already had seven husbands, and you were not named after any of them. Why do you beat us because of them? If they are dead, go be with them, and let us never see either a son or daughter from you."

When she heard these things she was very sad, and she thought of strangling herself, and she said, "I am the only daughter of my father, and if I do this, it will be a reproach against him, and I will bring his old age with sadness to the grave."

Then she prayed towards the window, and said, "Blessed are you, my Lord the god,[4] and your holy and glorious name is blessed and honorable forever. Let all your works praise you forever. Now, Lord, I set I my eyes and my face towards you, say, 'Take me out of the earth, that I may no longer hear the reproach.' You know, Lord, that I am pure from all sin with man, and that I never polluted my name, or the name of my father, in the land of my captivity. I am the only daughter of my father, and he has no child to be his heir, nor any near relative, or any son of his alive to whom I may offer myself to as a wife. My seven husbands are already dead, and why should I live? If it does not please you that I should die, command some thought to be had of me, and pity taken of me, that I hear no more insults."

The prayers of them both were heard before the majesty of the great God, and great (God and send Lord) Raphael (the messenger himself,)[5] was sent to heal them both, to remove the scales from the whiteness of Tobit's eyes, and to give Sarah the daughter of Raguel as a wife to Tobiah the son of Tobit, and to bind Asmodeus the evil spirit, because she belonged to Tobiah by right of inheritance. When Tobit came home and entered his house, Sarah the daughter of Raguel came down from her upper room.

Tobit (Vaticanus): Chapter 3 Notes

1 Codex Vaticanus: Ekbatanois (ЄКВΑΤΑΝΟΙС)

- LXX 243: Ecbasanoes (ЄιιιΛσΛνοιc)

- Codex Complutensis 1 (VL 109): Bethanis

- Ge'ez manuscripts: Bitani (ቢጣኒ)

Ecbatana was the capital of the Median Empire, and later the summer capital of the Persian Empire. Its name translates in old Persian as 'the place of gathering.'

2 Codex Vaticanus: Asmodaus (ΑСΜΟΔΑΥС)

- Codex Sinaiticus: Asmodeos (ΑСΜΟΔЄΟС)

- LXX 319: Asmodeus (ΑσμοΔόυc)

- LXX 46: Asmodaeon (Ασμοδαιον)

- Codex Bobbiensis (VL 135): Asmadeum

- Codex Complutensis 1 (VL 109): Nasbodeus

Asmodeus is a Jewish and Samaritan demon, adopted from the Zoroastrian faith. The name is derived from the Avestan aēšəma daēuua (𐬀𐬉𐬱𐬆𐬨𐬀 𐬛𐬀𐬉𐬎𐬎𐬀), which translates as wrath-demon. At the time, Zoroastrianism was one of the religions practiced in Media.

3 Codex Vaticanus: to ponêron daemonion (ΤΟΠΟΝΗΡΟΝ ΔΑΙΜΟΝΙΟΝ). Translation: the wrathful (or painful, oppressive, grievous) demon (or divine, lesser god, powerful spirit)

• Codex Sinaiticus: to daemonion to ponêron (ΤΟ ΔΑΙΜΟΝΙΟΝ ΤΟ ΠΟΝΗΡΟΝ). Translation: the demon (or divine, lesser god, powerful spirit) the wrathful (or painful, oppressive, grievous)

The Greek term has many interpretations, and at its core relates to something powerful. As the being in question was a Zoroastrian demon, the original term used in the Aramaic text was likely and Aramaic translation of the Avestan term aēšəma daēuua (ܐܝܫܡܐ_ܘ ܕܐܝܘܘܐ), which translates as 'wrath demon.'

4 Codex Vaticanus: Cyrie o theos (ΚΥΡΙΕΟΘΕΟC). Translation: lord the god

• LXX 126: Cyrios o theos (Κυριος ο θεος). Translation: lord the god

Based on the Aramaic sections of Masoretic Daniel that were not translated into Hebrew, the original Aramaic term the Greeks translated as 'Lord the god' was almost certainly adonai ha'elohim (אֲדֹנָי הָאֱלֹהִים), which in Aramaic means 'lord of the gods,' however, interpreted in Neo-Assyrian or Neo-Babylonian means 'lord the god.'

5 Codex Vaticanus: megalou Raphaêl (ΜΕΓΑΛΟΥ ΡΑΦΑΗΛ). Translation: great Raphael

• LXX 126: megalou Theos cae apestile Cyrios Raphaêl ton angelon autou (μεγαλου Θεος και απεστιλε Κυριος Ραφαηλ τον ἀγγόλον ἀυτου). Translation: great god and sent Lord Raphael the messenger himself

- LXX 311: megalou apestal Raphaêl (μόγαλου ἀπόοταλ ΡΑϦΑλλ λ). Translation: great apostle Raphael

Raphael was a messenger in some Judahites sects and later adopted by Christians and Muslims. Raphael only appears in the books of Tobit and the Watchers (1st Enoch). Both seem to have been important to Essen communities later, and neither was of interest to the Pharisees or Sadducees. As Josephus claimed the Essenes considered themselves to be descents of the ancient Canaanites, it is plausible that this name started as a reference to a healing god.

Tobit (Vaticanus): Chapter 4

On that day, Tobit remembered the silver that he had committed to Gabael in the city of Ray in Media, and said to himself, "I have wished for death, therefore, I will call for my son Tobiah that I may sign over to him of the silver before I die."

He called him and he said, "My son when I am dead, bury me, and don't neglect your mother, but honor her all the days of your life, and do that which will please her, and do not grieve her. Remember, my son, that she saw many dangers for you when you were in her womb, and when she is dead, bury her next to me in the same grave."

"My son, be mindful of our Lord the god all your days and don't let your will be set to sin or to transgress his commandments. Do correctly all your life, and don't follow the ways of unrighteousness. If you deal honestly, your business will prosper and you will succeed."

"Give to charities from your property, and when you give charitably, don't let your eye be envious, nor turn your face from any of the poor, and the face of God will not be turned away from you."

"If you have abundance give charitably accordingly, but if you have but a little, do not be afraid to give according to that little. You lay up a good treasure for yourself against the day of necessity. Because that charity delivers from death and allows not to come into darkness. Charity is a good gift to all that give it in the sight of the Highest."

"Beware of all whores my son, and make sure to take a wife from one of your relatives, and don't take a foreign woman as a wife, who is not of your father's tribe. We are the children of the prophets, Noah, Abraham, Isaac, and Jacob. Remember, my son, that our fore-fathers from the beginning, they all married wives of their own families, and were blessed in their children, and their seed will inherit the land."

"Now, therefore, my son, love your brothers and don't despise in your heart your brothers, the sons, and daughters of your people, in not taking a wife of them. In pride comes, destruction and much trouble, and in lewdness is decay and great lack, for lewdness is the mother of famine."

"Don't let the wages of any man, who has worked for you remain with you, but give him it out of hand, for if you serve God, he will also repay you. Be circumspect my son, in all things you do, and be wise in all your conversation. Don't do that which you hate to any man."

"Don't drink wine until you are drunken, nor let drunkenness go with you in your journey. Give of your bread to the hungry, and of your garments to them that are naked, and according to your abundance give charitably.

"Don't let your eye be envious when you give to charity. Pour out your bread on the burial of the just, but give nothing to the wicked. Ask counsel of all that are wise, and don't despise any profitable counsel."

"Bless your Lord the god always, and desire of him that your ways may be directed, and that all your paths and counsels may prosper, for every nation has no counsel, but the Lord himself gives all good things, and he humbles whom he will, as he will."

"Now, therefore, my son, remember my commandments, neither let them be put out of your mind. I signify this to them, that I committed ten talents to Gabael ben Gabri at Ray in Media. Don't be afraid, my son, that we are made poor, for you have much wealth, if you fear God, and leave from all sin, and do that which is pleasing in his sight."

Tobit (Vaticanus): Chapter 5

Tobiah answered him, "Father, I will do all things which you have commanded me. But how can I receive the silver, seeing I do not know him?"

Then he gave him the handwritten message, and said to him, "Find a man who will go with you, while I yet live, and I will pay him wages. Then go and receive the silver."

Therefore, when he went to seek the man, he found Raphael, who was a messenger.[1] He did not know, and he asked him, "Can you go with me to Ray? Do you know the place well?"

The messenger answered, "I will go with you, and I know the road well, as I have lodged with our brother Gabael."

Then Tobiah told him, "Wait for me until I tell my father."

He replied to him, "Go, and don't delay."

He went in and said to his father, "Look, I have found one who will go with me."

Then he stated, "Call him to me, that I may know of what tribe he is, and whether he is a trustworthy man to go with you."

So he called him, and he came in, and they greeted one another. Then Tobit asked him, "Brother, tell me of what tribe and family you are."

He answered, "Are you looking for a tribe or family, or a hired man to go with your son?"

Then Tobit said to him, "I would know, brother, your families, and name."

Then he answered, "I am Azariah, the son of Hananiah the great, and of your brothers."

Then Tobit replied, "You are welcome, brother. Do not be angry with me, because I have inquired to know your tribe and your family, for you are my brother, of an honest and good stock. I know Hananiah and Iathan, sons of that great Shemaiah, as we went together to Jerusalem to worship, and offered the firstborn, and the tenths of the fruits, and they were not seduced with the error of our brothers. My brother, you are of good stock. But tell me, what wages will I give you? Will you take a beka^2 a day, and costs equal to my son's?"

"Yes."

"Also, if you return safe, I will add a bonus to your wages."

So they were very pleased, and he said to Tobiah, "Prepare yourself for the journey, and God send you on a good journey."

When his son had prepared all things for the journey, his father said, "Travel with this man, and Shamayim Baitylos[3] will bring success to your journey, and his messenger will accompany you."

So they left together, along with the young man's dog, but Hannah his mother wept, and asked Tobit, "Why have you sent away our son? Is he not the staff of our hand, going in and out before us? Do not be greedy to add silver to silver, but let it be as garbage in comparison to our child, Amen![4] For that which the Lord has given us to live with is enough for us."

Tobit replied to her, "Don't worry, my sister, he will return in safety, and your eyes will see him. For the good messenger will keep him company, and his journey will be prosperous, and he will return safe," and so she stopped crying.

Tobit (Vaticanus): Chapter 5 Notes

1 Codex Vaticanus: angelos (ᴀⲅⲅⲉⲗⲟⲥ). Translation: messenger

- Codex Sinaiticus: angelos tou theou (ᴀⲅⲅⲉⲗⲟⲥⲧⲟⲩ ⲑⲉⲟⲩ). Translation: messenger of the god

- LXX 236: angelon (ἀγγἐλον). Translation: messenger

- LXX 71: angelos Cyriou (ἀγγἐλος Κυρίου). Translation: messenger of Lord

2 Codex Vaticanus: drachmên (ⲇⲣⲁⲭⲙⲏⲛ)

- Codex Corbeiensis (VL 150): didragmam

The drachma was a Greek coin used from around 1100 BC, worth approximately 4.3 grams of silver. The name drachma was used in the Septuagint as a translation for the beka (בֶּקַע), was the half-shekel measurement used in ancient Canaan. As 'drachma' was the Greek translation of beka, the term beka is restored.

3 Codex Vaticanus: ouranô oecôn theos (ⲟⲩⲣⲁⲛⲱⲟⲓⲕⲱⲛ ⲑⲉⲟⲥ). Translation: Uranus (or sky) house god

- Codex Sinaiticus: theos o en tô ouranô (ⲑⲉⲟⲥⲟⲉⲛⲧⲱ ⲟⲩⲣⲁⲛⲱ). Translation: god that is the Uranus (or sky)

The proper name of Uranus is used in this version of the Septuagint, however, could not have been in the Aramaic source text the Greeks used. The name is also found in other versions of Tobit, such as the Codex Sinaiticus' version, and so it is likely that it was in the original Greek translation. The early-Israelite version of Uranus was Shamayim, which may have been in the original Aramaic text, however, the following two words oecôn theos (οἰκῶν θεὸς) were used as a Greek translation for Bethel (𐡁𐡉𐡕𐡀𐡋), which was the name of an earlier Canaanite sky-god, widely worshiped in Samaria, where his major religious center was located: Bethel. Based on the writings of Jeremiah and Baruch, the god Bethel continued to be worshiped in Judah until the kingdom was conquered by the Babylonians.

The Canaanite god Bethel, whose name means 'house of god,' was widely worshiped across Canaan, Anatolia, and the Aegean during the late bronze-age, and was likely a version of the Egyptian goddess Hathor, whose name meant 'House of Ra.' Based on Baruch's description of his god, the god in question was Shemesh, the Canaanite sun-god, which mirrors the role of Ra in the Egyptian pantheon. The alternate name of Bethel in modern literature, Baitylos, is derived from Sanchuniathon's Phoenician History, which was originally published sometime in the late bronze age. Baitylos is used to differentiate the god from the town named after him, however, both were pronounced the same in ancient Canaanite, Aramaic, and Hebrew. Bethel was also the word for 'meteorite,' and shrines dedicated to Baitylos were built as meteorite impact sites across the Mediterranean, and continued to be worshiped in Northwest Africa as late as the 5th century AD.

As Uranus was a translation, presumably of Shamayim, and 'house god' is clearly a translation of Baitylos, Shamayim Baitylos is used in this translation. These names were also used interchangeably by Jeremiah and Baruch.

Tobit (Vaticanus): Chapter 6

As they traveled on their journey they traveled down the Tigris River, and one evening they camped on the bank. When the young man went down to wash, a fish leaped out of the river and would have eaten him, but the messenger shouted to him, "Catch the fish!"

The young man grabbed hold of the fish and pulled it onto land, and the messenger said, "Cut open the fish, and take the heart and the liver and the guts, and keep them safe."

So the young man did as the messenger commanded him, and when they had roasted the fish, they ate it, then they both went on their way until they arrived at Ecbatana. Then the young man asked the messenger, "Brother Azariah, to what use is the heart and the liver and the guts of the fish?"

He said to him, "Touch the heart and the liver, if a demon or a destructive spirit[1] troubles you in any way. If we smoke them before a man or woman, the party will no longer be cursed. As for the guts, it is good to anoint a man that has whiteness in his eyes, and he will be healed."

When they had come close to Ray, the messenger said to the young man, "Brother, today we will lodge with Raguel, who is your cousin. He has only one daughter, named Sarah. I will ask for her, that she may be given to you as a wife. You have the right to claim her, seeing you are the only one of her family left. The girl is good-looking and wise. Now, hear me and I will speak to her father, and when we return from Ray we will celebrate the marriage. I know that Raguel can't marry her to another according to the law of Moses, as he will be guilty of death, because the right of inheritance applies to you rather than to any other."

Then the young man answered the messenger, "I have heard, brother Azariah that this girl has been given to seven men, who all died in the marriage chamber. Now, I am my father's only son, and I am afraid, in case if I go into her, I will die, like the others before me. A wicked spirit loves her, which hurts anybody who comes to her. Therefore, I also fear in case I die, and bring my father's and my mother's life to the grave with sorrow because of me, for they have no other son to bury them."

Then the messenger said to him, "Don't you remember the commands which your father gave you, that you should marry a wife of your own family? Therefore hear me, my brother, for she will be given to you as a wife, and don't be concerned about the evil spirit, for this very night will she be given you in marriage. When you will enter your bride, take the ashes of incense and will lay on them the heart and liver of the fish, and make a smoke with it. The demon will smell it, and flee, and not return for ages and ages. When you come to her, both of you rise and pray to the gracious god, to save you and have mercy on you. Have no fears, as she is appointed to you from the beginning. You will save her, and she will go with you, and she will carry your children."

Now when Tobiah had heard these things, he loved her, and his heart was effectually joined to her.

Tobit (Vaticanus): Chapter 6 Notes

1 Codex Vaticanus: daemonion ê paneuma ponêron (ⲆⲀⲓⲘⲞⲚⲓⲞⲚ Ⲏ ⲠⲀⲚⲈⲨⲘⲀ ⲠⲞⲚⲎⲣⲞⲚ). Translation: demon (or lesser god, powerful spirit, divinity) or (or as) spirit (or wind, breath, life, air, angel) destructive (or painful, grievous)

- Codex Sinaiticus: daemoniou ê pneumatos ponêrou (ⲆⲀⲓⲘⲞⲚⲓⲞⲨ Ⲏ ⲠⲚⲈⲨⲘⲀⲦⲞⲤ ⲠⲞⲚⲎⲣⲞⲨ). Translation: demon (or lesser god, powerful spirit, divinity) or (or as) spirit (or wind, breath, life, air, angel) destructive (or painful, grievous)

- LXX 71: daemonion (Δαιμονιον). Translation: demon (or lesser god, powerful spirit, divinity)

The phrase appears to originate in the Zoroastrian terms daeva (و_سـیسـ)), meaning 'demon,' and Angra Mainyu (سـیز۱سـ۰ٔ۶سـرٔسرٔ)), meaning 'destructive spirit.'

Tobit (Vaticanus): Chapter 7

When they arrived in Ecbatana, and reached the house of Raguel, Sarah met them, and after they had greeted one another, she brought them into the house. Then Raguel asked Edna his wife, "How much does this young man look like my cousin Tobit!"

Raguel asked them, "From where are you, brothers?"

They replied, "We are of the Naphtalites, which are captives in Nineveh."

Then he asked them, "Do you know Tobit our relative?"

They answered, "We know him."

Then he asked, "Is he in good health?"

They answered, "He is both alive, and in good health," and Tobiah added, "he is my father."

Then Raguel leaped up, and kissed him, and wept, blessed him, and said to him, "You are the son of an honest and good man!" But when he had heard that Tobit was blind, he was sad and wept, and Edna his wife, and also Sarah his daughter wept.

Nevertheless, they entertained them cheerfully, and after that, they killed a ram from the flock, and they set the meat on the table. Then Tobiah said to Raphael,

"Brother Azariah, speak of those things of which you talked along the road, and let this business be finished."

So he communicated the matter with Raguel, and Raguel said to Tobiah, "Eat and drink, and celebrate, for it is decided that you should marry my daughter! However, I will tell you the truth. I have given my daughter in marriage to seven men, who died the night they came into her. Nevertheless, for now, celebrate."

Tobiah replied, "I will eat nothing here, until we agree and swear one to another."

Raguel said, "Then take her from now on according to our custom, as you are her cousin, and she is yours, and the merciful God gave you good success in all things."

Then he called his daughter Sarah, and she came to her father, and he took her by the hand, and gave her to Tobiah as a wife, saying, "Look, take her according to the laws of Moses, and take her away to your father."

He blessed them, and called Edna his wife, and took a book and wrote a contract and sealed it. Then they began to eat. Afterward, Raguel called his wife Edna, and said to her, "Sister, prepare another room, and take her in there."

When she had done as he had ordered her, she brought her there, and she wept, and she received the tears of her daughter, and said to her, "Have courage, my child. The Lord of the sky and the earth give family to replace your sorrow, so be courageous my daughter."

Tobit (Vaticanus): Chapter 8

When they had eaten, they took Tobiah to her. As he went, he remembered the words of Raphael, and took the ashes of the incense, and put the heart and the liver of the fish on them, and smoked it. When the evil spirit smelled the odor, he fled for the farthest parts of Egypt, but the messenger caught him. When they were both behind closed doors, Tobiah rose out of the bed, and said, "Sister, rise, and let us pray that the Lord will have pity on us."

Then Tobiah prayed, "Blessed are you, god of our fathers, and blessed is your holy and glorious name forever. Let the skies bless you, and all your creatures. You made Adam and gave him Eve his wife as a helper, and from them came mankind. You said, 'It is not good that man should be alone, let us make for him a helper like himself.' Now, Lord, I do not take my sister like a prostitute, but uprightly, therefore mercifully ordain that we may become old together."

She said with him, "Amen."

So they slept together that night. Raguel arose, and went and dug a grave, saying, "I'm afraid that he is also dead." And when Raguel returned to his house, he told his wife Edna, "Send one of the girls, and let her see whether he is alive, if he is not, we can bury him before anyone finds out."

So the girl opened the door, and went in, and found them both asleep, and she returned and told them that he was alive. Then Raguel praised god, and said, "God, you are worthy to be praised with all pure and holy praise, therefore let your holy ones praise you with all your creatures, and let all your messengers and your elect praise you forever. You are to be praised, for you have made me joyful. It has not happened, that which I suspected, but you have dealt with us according to your great mercy. You are to be praised because you have had mercy on two that were the only begotten children of their fathers. Grant them mercy, Lord, and finish their life in health with joy and mercy."

Then Raguel commanded his servants to refill the grave. He kept the wedding feast fourteen days. For before the days of the marriage were finished, Raguel had said to him by an oath, that he should not leave until the fourteen days of the marriage were expired. Then he should take half of his goods, and go in safety to his father, and should have the rest, "when I and my wife are dead."

Tobit (Vaticanus): Chapter 9

Then Tobiah called Raphael, and said to him, "Brother Azariah, take with you a servant, and two camels, and go to Ray in Media to Gabael, and bring me the silver, and bring him to the wedding. Raguel has sworn that I will not leave, yet my father counts the days, and if I am too long, he will be very concerned. So Raphael went out, and lodged with Gabael, and gave him the handwritten message, and he brought out bags which were sealed up and gave them to him. Early in the morning they went out both together and came to the wedding, and Tobiah blessed his wife.

Tobit (Vaticanus): Chapter 10

His father Tobit counted every day and when the days of the journey were up and they had not returned, then Tobit asked, "Are they delayed, or is Gabael dead, and there is no man to give him the silver?"

Therefore he was very sad, and his wife said to him, "My son is dead," as he had stayed away so long. She began to wail and said to him, "Now I care for nothing! My son! Since I have let you go, the light of my eyes!"

To which Tobit replied, "Be silent! Don't be worried as he is safe."

But she replied, "You be silent, and stop lying to me! My son is dead!"

She went out every day to the road they had left on, and ate no food throughout the day, and did not stop mourning her son Tobiah all night until the fourteen days of the wedding had expired, which Raguel had sworn that he should spend there. Then Tobiah said to Raguel, "Let me go, as my father and mother will be looking for me."

But his father-in-law said to him, "Remain with me, and I will send a message to your father, and they will tell him how you are doing."

But Tobiah answered, "No, let me go to my father."

Then Raguel rose and gave him Sarah, his wife, and half his property, slaves, livestock, and silver. He blessed them, and sent them away, saying, "The god of the sky gives you a prosperous journey, my children," and he said to his daughter, "Honor your father and your mother in law, which are now your parents, so I may hear good things of you," and he kissed her.

Edna said to Tobiah, "The Lord of the skies[1] return you, my dear brother, and grant that I may see your children through my daughter Sarah before I die, that I may rejoice before the Lord. Look, I am trusting my daughter to you, do not mistreat her."

After this, Tobiah went his way, praising God that he had given him a prosperous journey, and blessed Raguel and Edna his wife.

Tobit (Vaticanus): Chapter 10 Notes

1 Codex Vaticanus: o theos tou ouranou (ΟΘΕΟϹΤΟΥ ΟΥΡΑΝΟΥ). Translation: the god the vaulted-sky

- Codex Sinaiticus: o cyrios tou ourano (ΟΚΥΡΙΟϹΤΟΥ ΟΥΡΑΝΟ). Translation: the lord the vaulted-sky

- Codex Alexandrinus: o cyrios tou ourano (ΟΘΕΟϹΤΟΥ ΟΥΡΑΝΟΤΕΚΝΑ). Translation: the god of the vaulted-sky's child (or descendant)

- LXX 107: ho cyrios Theos tou ouranou (ο Lⲇⲃρλος Θ6ος του ουρλνου). Translation: the lord God of the sky

The vaulted-sky (Ουρανου) of early Greek cosmology was based on, or very similar to, the Shamayim of the ancient Canaanite and Israelite religions. The Shamayim was the first thing created in Genesis, right before Eretz (Earth).

Tobit (Vaticanus): Chapter 11

He traveled the roads until they arrived at Nineveh, and then Raphael said to Tobiah, "You know, brother, how you left your father. Let's hurry ahead of your wife, and prepare the house. Take the guts of the fish in your hand." So they went their way, along with the dog.

Hannah was sitting looking down the road for her son, and when she saw him coming, she said to his father, "Look, your son comes, along with the man that went with him!"

Then Raphael said, "I know, Tobiah, that your father will open his eyes. So anoint his eyes with the guts, and they will become itchy and he will rub them, and the whiteness will fall away, and he will see you."

Then Hannah ran out, and fell on the neck of her son, and said to him, "Now that I have seen you, my son, I am content to die from now on!"

They both wept. Tobit also went out towards the door and stumbled, but his son ran to him and took hold of his father, and he rubbed the guts on his fathers' eyes, saying, "Be hopeful my father."

When his eyes began to itch, he rubbed them, and the whiteness fell away from the corners of his eyes, and when he saw his son, he fell on his neck. He wept and said, "Blessed are you, God, and blessed is your name forever! Blessed are all your holy messengers! For you have scourged, and have taken pity on me! Look, I see my son Tobiah!"

His son went in celebrating, and told his father the great things that had happened to him in Media. Then Tobit went out to meet his daughter-in-law at the gate of Nineveh, rejoicing and praising God, and those who saw him go by marveled because his sight had been restored. But Tobiah gave thanks before them that God had mercy on him. When he approached Sarah his daughter-in-law, he blessed her saying, "You are welcome, daughter. Blessed is the God who has brought you to us, and blessed is your father and your mother."

There was joy among all his brothers who were in Nineveh. Ahikar and his nephew Nadan[1] came, and Tobiah's wedding was celebrated seven days with great joy.

Tobit (Vaticanus): Chapter 10 Notes

1 Codex Vaticanus: Nasbas (ⲚⲀⳤⲂⲀⳤ)

• Codex Sinaiticus: Nabad (ⲚⲀⲂⲀⲆ)

• LXX 71: Nabas (ⲚⲀⲩⲁⲥ)

• Sahidic manuscripts: Asbas (ⲁⳤⲃⲁⲥ)

• Codex Complutensis 1 (VL 190): Nabat

• Codex Regius (VL 148): Nabal

• Codex Monacensis (VL 130): Nadab

The name of the nephew is not standardized in the manuscripts. The nephew's name used in the surviving copies of the Words of Ahikar is Nadan, which is used in this translation as the copies of the Septuagint do not agree.

Tobit (Vaticanus): Chapter 12

Then Tobit called his son Tobiah and said to him, "My son, see that the man who went with you is paid, and you must give him a bonus."

Tobiah said to him, "Father, it won't hurt me to give him half of everything which I have brought, as he has brought me back to you in safety, and saved my wife, and brought the silver to me, and also healed you."

Then the old man said, "It is due to him," so he called the messenger, and he said to him, "Take half of all that you have brought, and leave in safety."

Then he took them both separately, and said to them, "Bless God, praise him, and exalt him, and thank him for the things which he has done to you in the sight of all that live. It is good to praise God, and exalt his name, and honorably to declare the works of God, and so don't be slow to praise him. It is good to keep private the secret of a king, but it is honorable to reveal the works of God. Do that which is good, and no evil will touch you. Prayer is good with fasting and charity and righteousness. A little with righteousness is better than much with unrighteousness."

"It is better to give charitably than to save up gold, for charity delivers from death, and will purge away all sin. Those who exercise charity and righteousness will be filled with life, but they who sin are enemies to their own life. Certainly, I will take nothing from you. For I said, 'It was good to keep private the secret of a king, but that it was honorable to reveal the works of God.'"

"Now, therefore, when you prayed, and Sarah your daughter-in-law, I brought your prayers before Qetesh,[1] and when you buried the dead, I was also with you. When you did not delay to rise and leave your dinner to go bury the dead, your good deed was not hidden from me, but I was with you. And so, God has sent me to heal you, and Sarah your daughter-in-law. I am Raphael, one of the seven holy messengers, which present the prayers of the saints, and which go in and out before the glory of Qetesh."

Then they were both troubled, and fell on their faces, for they were afraid. But he said to them, "Don't be afraid, for it will be well with you. Praise God, and do not ask any favor from me. By the will of our God I came, therefore praise him forever. All these days I appeared to you, but I did not eat or drink, as you were seeing a vision. Now, therefore, give God thanks, for I go up to him that sent me. Write all the things which were done in a book."

When they rose, they no longer saw him. Then they confessed the great and wonderful works of God, and how the messenger of the Lord had appeared to them.

Tobit (Vaticanus): Chapter 12 Notes

1 Codex Vaticanus: agiou (ᴀⲅⲓⲟⲩ). Translation: saint

• Codex Sinaiticus: doxês cyriou (ⲇⲟⲍⲏⲥⲕⲩⲣⲓⲟⲩ). Translation: glorious (or magnificent, splendorous) lord

• LXX 542: Theo (Θεο). Translation: God

The term hagiou (Ἁγίου) is used in the Septuagint, where the Masoretic texts retain the word Qetesh (קדש), which was the title of the Israelite goddess Asherah, whose worship would later be banned by the Judahite king Josiah.

Tobit (Vaticanus): Chapter 13

Tobit wrote a prayer of joy and said,

"Blessed is God that lives for ages, and blessed in his kingdom. For he punishes and has mercy. He leads down to the grave and brings up again. Neither are there any that can avoid his hand. Tell of him to the nations you Israelites, for he has scattered us among them. Declare his greatness and extol him before all the living, for he is our Lord, and he is the god of our father for ages. He will scourge us for our iniquities, and have mercy again, and will gather us out of all nations, among whom he has scattered us."

"If you turn to him with your whole heart, and with your whole mind, and deal honestly before him, then will he return to you, and will not hide his face from you. Praise Lord Sydyk,[1] and praise the king of ages. In the land of my captivity, I praise him and declare his might and majesty to a sinful nation. You returned sinners, sang of justice before him. Who knows if he will accept you, and have mercy on you?"

"I will extol my god, and my mind will praise the king of the sky,[2] and will rejoice in his greatness. Let all men speak, and let all praise him in Jerusalem. Jerusalem, the holy city, he will scourge you for your children's works and have mercy again on the sons of the righteous. Give praise to the Lord, for he is good, and praise the king of ages, that his tabernacle may be built in you again with joy, and let him make joyful there in you those that are captives, and love in you forever those that are miserable. Many nations will come from far to the name of Lord the god with gifts in their hands, gifts to the king of the sky, all generations will praise you with great joy. Cursed are all they who hate you, and blessed will all be which love you forever."

"Rejoice and be glad for the children of the just, for they will be gathered together, and will bless the Lord of the just. Blessed are they which love you, for they will rejoice in your peace, blessed are they which have been sorrowful for all your scourges, for they will rejoice for you, when they have seen all your glory, and will be glad forever. Let my mind bless the great god king.[3] For Jerusalem will be built up with sapphires and emeralds, and precious stone, your walls and towers and battlements with pure gold. The streets of Jerusalem will be paved with beryl and carbuncle and stones of Sauvira.[4] All her streets will say, 'Hallelujah,' and they will praise him, saying, 'Blessed is the god who has exalted you forever.'"

Tobit (Vaticanus): Chapter 13 Notes

1 Codex Vaticanus: ton cyrion tês dicaeosynês (ΤΟΝ ΚΥΡΙΟΝΤΗϹΔΙΚΑΙΟϹΥΝΗϹ). Translation: the lord the justice

- LXX 249: ton theon tês dicaeosynês (ΤΟΝ θ͞ο͞ν τ͡ηϲ ΔικΔιοσυν͡ηϲ). Translation: the god the justice

- Codex Corbeiensis (VL 150): de dominus in iustitia. Translation: the lord in (or under, towards) Justinia

- Codex Bobbiensis (VL 135): de deum de iustitiam. Translation: the god the justice

The term 'the justice' (τῆσ Δικαιοσύνης) was used in the Septuagint for places where the Masoretic Texts retains the name Sydyk (צֶדֶק), the Canaanite god of justice. During the Roman era, the same name was applied to the Roman god Jupiter (Iove) as well as for the Roman spirit of Justice (Iustitia) by Hebrew-speaking people, meaning the knowledge of Sydyk had not disappeared by the early Christian era.

2 Codex Vaticanus: basili tou ouranou (ΒΑϹΙΛΕΙΤΟΥ ΟΥΡΑΝΟΥ). Translation: king the vaulted-sky (or Uranus)

- Codex Complutensis 1 (VL109): regem de caelum. Translation: king of the sky

- Codex Bobbiensis (VL 135): rex de caelum et terrae. Translation: king of the sky and land

The vaulted-sky (Ουρανου) of early Greek cosmology was based on, or very similar to, the Shamayim of the ancient

Canaanite and Israelite religions, however, the term 'king' is more problematic, as the Aramaic word mlch (ﬡﬤﬥﬨ) is likely the source of the Septuagint's word Moloch, the name of one of the gods that Solomon set up an idol to in his temple.

The god in question was the Ammanite god mlk (ﬤﬥﬨ), whose name translates as king, however, the god's name is not pronounced in Hebrew as melech (מֶלֶךְ), meaning king, but preserves the Aramaic spelling as mwlch (מולך). This verse implies that Moloch was a title for Shamayim and Bethel, who certainly was a god being worshiped in the Temple in Jerusalem before King Josiah's reforms circa 625 BC, several decades after this book was apparently written.

3 Codex Vaticanus: ton theon ton basilea ton megan (ΤΟΝ ΘΕΟΝ ΤΟΝ ΒΑϹΙΛΕΑ ΤΟΝ ΜΕΓΑΝ). Translation: the god the king the great

• Codex Sinaiticus: ton cyrion ton basilea ton megan (ΤΟΝ ΚΥΡΙΟΝ ΤΟΝ ΒΑϹΙΛΕΑ ΤΟΝ ΜΕΓΑΝ). Translation: the god the king the great

• LXX 58: ton theon ton basilea ton mega (τον Θεον τον υΑσιλέα τον μέγα). Translation: the god the king the great

Given the pronunciation of 'king' in Aramaic, this may have read 'the god Moloch the great,' however, that cannot be proven with the surviving texts, and so a more generalized translation is used.

4 Codex Vaticanus: Souphir (ⲥⲟⲩⲫⲓⲣ)

- Codex Sinaiticus: Souphir (ⲥⲟⲩⲫⲉⲓⲣ)

- LXX 46: Ophir (Ο ϐⲟⲓⳍ)

- LXX 583: Saphir (ⲥⲁϐⲓⳍ)

- LXX 319: Souphêrô (ⲥⲟⲩϐⲗⳍⲟ)

- LXX 107: Souphêrô (ⲥⲟⲩϐⲗⳍ)

This quasi-mythical land of riches was also transliterated as Sophira (Σωφηρα) in other books of the Septuagint, and as Ofir (אוֹפִיר) in the Masoretic Texts.

The location of this civilization has been a matter of debate for ages. Given the list of items imported from Souphir/Sophira/Ofir, it was likely the ancient Pakistani Kingdom of Sauvira on the Indus River. Imported items include gold, silver, sandalwood, pearls, ivory, apes, and peacocks. Sandalwood trees are indigenous to South and Southeast Asia and have traditionally been considered sacred by the Hindus, Jainists, Buddhists, and Zoroastrians, as well as other Asian cultures. Peacocks are indigenous to South and Southeast Asia, as well as the Congo Rain-forest, however, Sandalwood trees are not found in the Congo Rain-forest. Apes were still living in South and Southeast Asia circa 1000 BC, along with most of Africa. An alternate theory regarding the location of Sophira was that it was a trading port in Southern Arabia or Somalia, however, the ships of Solomon were said to take three years to travel between Edom and

Souphir/Sophira/Ofir, which makes the location of Sauvira more likely.

The Kingdom of Sauvira is listed in the ancient Late Vedic period and early Buddhist literature, as well as the Mahabharata, based around its capital of Rohri in the modern Pakistani state of Sindh.

This civilization is recorded as having existed from the Early Vedic period, before 1100 BC, meaning it would have existed in the time of Solomon. The capital of Sauvira was Aror, also called Roruka or Rorik in classical literature, which was one of the most important cities in South Asia in the 7th century BC, when this book was set. According to the Buddhist Bhallatiya Jataka, as well as Jain Story of Udayan and the town of Vitabhaya, the city of Aror was destroyed by a major sandstorm around 450 BC, following which the modern city of Rorhi (روهڙي / روهڙی) was founded around 10 kilometers away.

Tobit (Vaticanus): Chapter 14

Tobit finished praising God.

He was 58 years old when he lost his sight, which was restored to him after 8 years.[1] He gave charitably, and he increased in his respect for Lord the god and praised him. When he was very old he called his son, and the sons of his son, and said to him, "My son, take your children, for look, I am old, and am ready to leave this life. Go into Media my son, for I certainly believe those things which Jonah the prophet said of Nineveh, that it will be overthrown.[2]

That for a time peace will be in Media, and that our brothers will lie scattered in the earth from that good land, and Jerusalem will be desolate, and the Temple of God in it will be burnt and will be desolate for a time, so again God will have mercy on them, and bring them back into the land, where they will build a temple, but not like the first, until the time of that age is finished, and afterward, they will return from all places of their captivity, and build up Jerusalem gloriously, and the Temple of God will be built in it forever with a glorious building, as the prophets have spoken of.

All nations will turn, and fear Lord the god truly, and will bury their idols, and the nations will praise the Lord, and his people will confess God, and the Lord will exalt his people, and all those which love Lord the god in truth and justice will rejoice, showing mercy to our brothers.

Now, my son, leave Nineveh because those things which the prophet Jonah spoke will certainly happen. But follow the law and the commandments, and show yourself merciful and just, that it may go well with you. Bury me decently, and your mother with me, but remain no longer in Nineveh."

"Child, remember what they did to Nadan.[3] Ahikar,[4] nursed him, yet he brought him out of the light into darkness, and what he returned to him, and Ahikar did not save him, but to him the repayment was given, and he went down into darkness. Manasseh[5] gave charitably, and escaped the snares of death which they had set for him, but Nadan[6] fell into the snare and perished. Therefore now, my son, consider what charity does, and how righteousness does deliver."

When he had said these things, he died in the bed at 158 years old, and he buried him honorably. When Hannah his mother was dead, he buried her with his father. Then Tobiah departed with his wife and children to Ecbatana to Raguel his father-in-law, where he became old with honor, and he buried his father and mother in law honorably, and he inherited their property, and his father Tobit's. He died at Ecbatana in Media, being 127 years old. But before he died he heard of the destruction of Nineveh, which was taken by Nebuchadnezzar and Xerxes,[7] and before his death, he rejoiced over Nineveh.

Tobit (Vaticanus): Chapter 14 Notes

1 Based on the chronology within the story, as Tobit lost his sight in 681 BC, and therefore this was the year 673 BC.

2 Codex Vaticanus: Iônas (ιⲱⲛⲁⲥ)

• Codex Sinaiticus: Naoum (ⲛⲁⲟⲩⲙ)

Both Nahum and Jonah predicted the destruction of Nineveh. The Book of Nahum is internally dated sometime during and shortly after the Assyrian occupation of Egypt between 663 and 656 BC, and generally accepted as dating to that era, while Jonah is widely regarded as being fiction by historians.

The Book of Jonah is internally dated sometime during the Assyrian rule of Samaria, approximately 720 to 612 BC. If Jonah and Tobit were both real people, they would have been in Nineveh at the same time, and given the size of the Samaritan population in Nineveh, likely would have met.

3 Codex Vaticanus: Adam (ⲁⲇⲁⲙ)

• Codex Sinaiticus: Nadab (ⲛⲁⲇⲁⲃ)

• LXX 535: Adad (ⲁⲇⲇⲇ)

• LXX 670: Naman (ⲛⲇⲙⲇⲛ)

• Sahidic manuscripts: Adar (ⲇⲇⲇⲣ)

• Codex Monacensis (VL 130): Nabad

• Codex Complutensis 1 (VL 109): Nabat

- Codex Bobbiensis (VL 135): Nabath

4 Codex Vaticanus: Achiacharô (ⲀⲬⲒⲀⲬⲀⲢⲱ)

- Codex Sinaiticus: Achicarô (ⲀⲬⲈⲒⲔⲀⲢⲱ)

- LXX 670: Achiacharou (Ⲁⲭⲓⲁⲭⲁⲣⲟⲩ)

- LXX 319: Agiacharô (Ⲁⲅⲓⲁⲭⲁⲣⲱ)

- Sahidic manuscripts: Akhiaros (ⲁ̄ⲭⲓⲁⲣⲟⲥ)

- Codex Complutensis 1 (VL 109): Acicarum

- Codex Bobbiensis (VL 135): Achicharo

5 Codex Vaticanus: Manassês (ⲘⲀⲚⲀⲤⲤⲎⲤ)

- Codex Sinaiticus: Nadab (Ⲛⲁⲁⲁⲩ)

- Codex Monacensis (VL 130): Nabad

- Codex Complutensis 1 (VL 109): Nabat

- Codex Bobbiensis (VL 135): Nabath

King Manasseh, who ruled Judah roughly between 687 and 643 BC, was mentioned in the records of the Assyrian kings Sennacherib, Esarhaddon, and Ashurbanipal, all of which consider Judah a vassal state. According to 2nd Paralipmenon (Masoretic Diḇrê Hayyāmîm), King Manasseh was at one point taken to Assyria in chains for some offense, and later restored to throne of Judah. This is believed to have happened during Esarhaddon's rule, between 681 and 669 BC.

It is unclear why Manasseh was mentioned in this verse in most versions of the Septuagint, however, he is not in the corresponding verse in the Sinaiticus version of Tobit, which claims Ahikar gave to charity, not Manasseh. Manasseh may have been a later insertion into the text, like Nebuchadnezzar and Ahasuerus, who are mentioned later in the chapter, in the Vaticanus version, but not the Sinaiticus version, which maintains the correct name of King Cyaxarês.

6 Codex Vaticanus: Adam (ⲁⲇⲁⲙ)

- Codex Sinaiticus: Nadab (ⲚⲀⲆⲀⲃ)

- LXX 535: Adad (ⲁⲇⲇⲇ)

- Sahidic manuscripts: Adas (ⲇⲇⲁⲥ)

7 Codex Vaticanus: Nabouchodonosor cae Asyêros (ⲚⲀⲃⲞⲨⲬⲞⲇⲞⲚⲞⲤⲞⲢⲔⲀⲓⲀⲤⲨⲎⲢⲞⲤ). Translation: Nabouchodonosor and Asyeros

- Codex Sinaiticus: Achiacharos (ⲀⲬⲉⲓⲀⲬⲀⲢⲞⲤ)

- Codex Alexandrinus: Nabouchodonosor cae Asouchros (ⲚⲀⲃⲞⲨⲬⲞⲇⲞⲚⲞⲤⲞⲢⲔⲀⲓⲀⲤⲞⲨⲬⲢⲞⲤ). Translation: Nabouchodonosor and Asouchros

- LXX 319: Nabouchodonosor cae Assyêros (Νⲇⲙⲟⲩⲭⲟⲇⲟⲛⲟⲥⲟⲣ ⲓⲇⲓ Ⲁⲥⲟⲩⲗ̄ⲣⲟⲥ). Translation: Nabouchodonosor and Assyeros

- LXX 46: Nabouchodonosor cae Asoêros (Νᴧμουχοᴧονοσοβ ᴜᴧι ᴧσοᴜβος). Translation: Nabouchodonosor and Asoeros

- LXX 488: Nabouchodonosor cae Assoucros (Νᴧμουχοᴧονοσοβ ᴜᴧι ᴧσσουᴜβος). Translation: Nabouchodonosor and Assoucros

This final line appears to be part of an anachronistic redaction. The Babylonian King Nabopolassar sacked Nineveh in 612 BC, along with Median and Persian allies. His son Nebuchadnezzar, who assumed the throne in 605 BC, finally conquered the remnants of the Assyrian forces in Syria at the Battle of Carchemish that same year, however, he did not destroy Nineveh. The name Asyêros (Ασυηρος) is generally accepted as a variant spelling of Ahasuerus (Ασουηρος), the Aramaic name of Xerxes, the Persian king who ruled between 486 and 465 BC.

The Codex Sinaiticus' does not mention either king, but gives credit to King Achiacharos (Αχιαχαρος) of Media, which is likely an attempt to transliterate the name Uvaxštra (𒀭𒆠𒌋𒅅𒍝𒎙𒂊), which was also transliterated as Cyaxarês (Κυαξάρης) in Greek, from which his common English name is derived. Other ancient versions of his name include the Elamite Makiišturri (𒇽𒈦𒁹𒀀𒋫𒊑), Neo-Babylonian Úaksatar (𒈨𒄩𒆪𒊓𒋻𒀪), and the Phrygian Ksuwaksaros (ΚΣΟꟼΑΥϞΡΟϚ). Cyaxares was the Median king who fought alongside the Babylonian King Nabopolassar at the sack of Nineveh, following which Nineveh became part of his

Median Empire. This seems clear proof that the Codex Sinaiticus version of Tobit is older, and more accurate.

Tobit (Sinaiticus): Chapter 1

The book of the words of Tobit,[1] the son of Tobiel, the son of Ananiel, the son of Aduel, the son of Gabael, the son of Raphael, the son of Raguel, of the descendants of Asahel, of the tribe of Naphtali, who in the time of King Sargon II[2] of the Assyrians was led captive out of Tishbe,[3] which is to the right of Kadesh of Naphtali in Galilee near Asher, back along the roadway to the westward sun, on the left of Peor.[4]

I, Tobit, have followed all the days of my life in the ways of truth and justice, and I was very charitable to my brothers from my nation, who came with me as captives to Nineveh in the land of the Assyrians. When I was still young in my own country of Israel, all of my father's tribe of Naphtali abandoned the house of David of my father, and Jerusalem,[5] which was chosen out of all the tribes of Israel that all the tribes should sacrifice there, where the temple and tabernacle[6] of God[7] was consecrated and built for all ages.[8]

All of my brothers and the house of Naphtali, my father, sacrificed to the young calf created by Jeroboam the king of Israel in Dan and on every mountain in Galilee.[9]

I regularly went by myself to Jerusalem at the feasts, as it was ordained to all Israel by an eternal decree, that the first-born, and the first-fruits, and tithe of the animals. The first-born of the sheep I drove to Jerusalem and gave to the priests, the sons of Aaron, for the altar. The tithe of grain, wine, oil, pomegranates, figs, and the rest of the best fruits, I gave to the Levites who served in Jerusalem. A second tenth I would spend on everything in Jerusalem, each year. What was left I gave to the orphans and the widows, and to the proselytes[10] living among the Israelites I contributed to them a third each year, and I ate everything following the ordinances, the commandments about this in the law of Moses, and following the orders of Debora the mother of Ananiel, my father, as I was orphaned when my father was crushed and died.

When I had come to the age of a man, I took a wife from the descendants of our race, and fathered a son through her, and called his name Tobiah. When we were taken prisoners by the Assyrians, and forced to be captives in Nineveh, all of my brothers and those of my tribes, ate the food of the nations, but I didn't. I kept my mind, and did not eat the food of the nations, as I remembered my god in my mind.

The Highest gave me grace and favor before Sargon II, so that I became the purchaser of his provisions, and I was sent to Media[11] frequently in the years before he died. Once, I gave Gabael the brother of Garbi, in the land of Media a bag containing ten talents of silver.

When Sargon II was dead, Sennacherib[12] his son reigned in his place, and the roads to Media were closed and there was no longer any way to travel to Media. In the days of Sargon, I was very charitable to my brothers of my tribes, and gave my bread to the hungry, my clothes to the naked, and if I saw any of my nation dead, or thrown out of the walls of Nineveh, I buried him.

If Sennacherib killed any, when he came back from Judea, in the days of the judgment he made for the king of the sky,[13] against blasphemers and those that spoke profanely of sacred things, I buried them. He killed many of the Israelites in his anger, and their bodies were buried honorably, and looked for by Sennacherib, but not found.

When one of the Ninevites went and told the king about me, that I buried them, I hid, knowing that I was being searched for, as the king wanted me executed, and I fled in fear. Then all my property was seized and there was nothing left to me. All the nobles abandoned me, other than my wife Hannah and my son Tobiah.

Less than forty days passed, before two of his sons killed him,[14] and they fled into the mountains of Urartu,[15] and Esarhaddon[16] his son reigned in his place, who had with him Ahikar[17] my brother Anael's son, who had under his reckoning the entire kingdom, and held the office over the administrators. Ahikar asked about me, and I returned to Nineveh. Ahikar was chief cupbearer, and keeper of the signet, and commander, and accountant, for King Sennacherib of Assyria, and became second to Esarhaddon, and he was my cousin, and from my family.

Tobit (Sinaiticus): Chapter 1 Notes

1 Codex Sinaiticus: Tobith (ⲦⲰⲂⲒⲐ)

- Codex Vaticanus: Tôbit (ⲦⲰⲂⲈⲒⲦ)

- LXX 106: Tôbit (ⲦⲟⲟⲩⲓⲦ)

- LXX 248: Tôbêt (Ⲧⲟⲟⲩⲏⲧ)

- LXX 392: Tôbid (ⲦⲟⲟⲩⳟⲓⲀ)

The names in the various manuscripts of the book of Tobit/Tobith/Tobid are not standardized, including the names of the book itself. This indicates three or more separate translations into Greek, as no one would have a reason to change the names if redacting one to make the other. The more common English name 'Tobit' is used in this translation.

2 Codex Sinaiticus: Enemessarou (ⲈⲚⲈⲘⲈⲤⲤⲀⲢⲞⲨ)

- LXX 46: Ennemesarou (Ἐννεμεσάρου)

- LXX 71: Enemesarou (Ἐνεμεσάρου)

- LXX 318: Enaimesarou (Ἐναιμεσάρου)

- LXX 122: Enemesarrou (Ἐνεμεσάρρου)

- LXX 249: Enemassarou (Ἐνεμασσάρου)

- LXX 107: Nemessarou (Νεμεσσάρου)

- Sahidic manuscripts: Namessaros (Ⲛⲁⲙⲉⲥⲥⲁⲣⲟⲥ)

Based on the rest of the book this must be a reference to Sargon II, King of Assyria between 722 and 705 BC. The name is often mistranslated as Shalmaneser, however, Enemessarou's son is later identified as Sennacherib, who was Sargon II's son. Shalmaneser was recorded in the books of the Kingdoms (Masoretic Kings), as having conquered Samaria, however, while Shalmaneser V's armies did besiege Samaria for three years, he died before Samaria surrendered, and when they surrendered, it was to Sargon II, Shalmaneser V's heir, who recorded in his records that he deported 27,920 Samaritans to Assyria.

This appears to have been an Aramaic translation of his Assyrian name Šarru-kīnum (𒈗𒁀𒆕𒌷), with the Assyrian terms inverted to Kīnum-šarru. His name is believed to translate as approximately as 'king who is legitimate,' suggesting the Aramaic translator interpreted then name as 'legitimate king,' and was not basing the reference on a historic record of the king, after his throne name had become standardized, but lived in the era of Sargon II.

Assuming this is a reference to Sargon, which it appears to be, it is notable that in the Book of Isaiah, the name Šarru-kīnum is rendered as Sargôn (סַרְגוֹן), meaning that the Book of Tobit is not dependent on Isaiah, and was likely translated into Aramaic by someone who had not read Isaiah. This supports the author's claims to be a Samaritan living in Assyria, and the dating of the text to the era of the Assyrian

Empire. The Hebrew-derived name 'Sargon' is used in this translation, as it is more common in modern English.

3 Codex Sinaiticus: Tishbes (ⲈⲒ�ⲤⲂⲎⳞ)

- Codex Alexandrinus: Thêbês (ⲐⲎⲂⲎⳞ)

- Peshitta: Thbhš (ܬܒܚܫ). Translation: Thebes

- Codex Corbeiensis (VL 150): Bibel

- Codex Sangermanensis 4 (VL 7 : Viel

- Codex Complutensis 1 (VL 109): Biel

- Codex Monacensis (VL 130): Cibiel

- Codex Bobbiensis (VL 135): Sibiel

- Ge'ez ms.: Tebesi (ጤቤሲ). Translation: Thebes

The Vaticanus and Sinaiticus manuscripts agree that is was the accepted Greek translation of the town called Tishbe (תִּשְׁבֶּ) in Hebrew, however, not all biblical scholars agree that there was a town called Tishbe in the Masoretic Texts. The issue revolves around the meaning of the word tishbi (תִּשְׁבִּי), which could simply be interpreted as 'resident,' however, was traditionally interpreted as Tishbite, meaning someone from Tishbe. The prophet Elijah was recorded as being a Tishbite, or maybe a 'resident,' in the Masoretic Kings (3rd Kingdoms) chapter 17.

The Septuagint's translation is clearer, where he is recorded as being a Tishbite from Tishbe (Θεσβίτης ἐκ Θεσβων), and so this translation accepts the traditional interpretation of the name Tishbe. It is significant though, that Elijah was closely connected with the Assyrian Samaritans on the Khabur River, where he saw the cherubs and the flying chariot in the cloud of fire and lightning. If he was from the same town as those relocated by Sargon II, it would make sense for him to visit them, as they would have been his cousins.

A large number of Greek, Latin, Syriac, and Ge'ez manuscripts deviate on this name, with the largest alternate reading being Thebes. It is unclear if this was intended to represent Thebes in Egypt, or Greece, or another town in the mind of the translator. Thebes was a city in Greece at the time, however, the city later renamed Thebes in Egypt, was still known as was still known as Wôst (𓏏).

The name Thêbês (ⲐⲎⲃⲎⲤ) in the Codex Vaticanus, and Thebes (ⲐⲈⲃⲈⲤ) in the Codex Alexandrinus, was also used as a translation for a name of a town in Canaan in the book of Judges chapter 9. The town's name is rendered as Tbṣ (תבץ) in the Aleppo Codex, and Tēbēṣ (תֵּבֵץ) in the Leningrad Codex, and is generally accepted as being Tubas (طوباس) in the northern area of the modern Palestinian West Bank. As this is in the region where Tishbe (תִּשְׁבֵּ) was supposed to have been located, it is possible that both names refer to the same town.

4 Codex Sinaticus: Phogôr (ⲫⲟⲅⲱⲣ)

- Codex Monacensis (VL 130): Raphain

- Codex Corbeiensis (VL 150): Raphaim

Phogôr (Φογωρ) appears to be a variant spelling of Phagôr (Φαγὼρ), mentioned in the Septuagint's Joshua, and translated as Peor (פְּעוֹר) in the Masoretic Texts. As all three towns, Phogôr, Phagôr, and Peor are reported as being in the same general location, it does seem likely that this was a variant transliteration of Peor through Aramaic into Greek, and so the name Peor is used in this translation.

The Vetus Latina codices all use either Raphian or Raphiam, which are two alternate transliterations of the name Refa'im (רְפָאִים) from the Masoretic Texts. The term was transliterated as Raphaen (Ραφαιν) in the Septuagint, however, not in any surviving copies of the book of Tobit, suggesting the Vetus Latina manuscripts all descend from a non-Greek source text. The differences in transliteration between Raphain and Raphaim, used in different versions of the old Latin Tobit, may indicate two separate sources, as the word was spelled Rpåym (רפאים) in Hebrew and Rpåm (𐤓𐤐𐤀𐤌) in Phoenician, or Rpåyn (𐡓𐡐𐡀𐡉𐡍) in Aramaic and Raphain (Ⲣⲁⲫⲁⲓⲛ) in Coptic.

5 Codex Sinaiticus: oecou Dauid tou patros mou cae apo Ierousalêm (ΟΙΚΟΥ ⲆⲀⲨⲈⲓⲆ ΤΟΥ ΠⲀΤⲢΟⲤ ⲘΟΥ ΚⲀⲓ ⲀΠΟ ⲓⲉⲢΟΥⳠⲀⲀⲎⲘ). Translation: house of David of my father and from Jerusalem

• Codex Vaticanus: oecou Ierosolymôn (ΟΙΚΟΥ ⲓⲉⲢΟⳠΟⲀΥⲘⳠⲚ). Translation: house of Jerusalem, temple in Jerusalem

TOBIT (SINAITICUS): CHAPTER 1 NOTES

The Codex Sinaiticus version is more political than the Vaticanus version, focused in the House of David, and the city of Jerusalem, instead of the temple specifically, although that is important too, and is referenced in the rest of the sentence in both versions. The focus on David is more commonly found in Aramaic texts than Hebrew, where the Kingdom of Judah was commonly referred to as the Kingdom of David.

6 Codex Sinaiticus: catascênôseôs (ΚΑΤΑϹΚΗΝѠϹΕѠϹ). Translation: camping place

This is most likely an attempt to translate 'tabernacle' into Greek via Aramaic, and so the more common term is used in this translation.

7 Codex Sinaiticus: theou (ѲΕΟΥ). Translation: god

• Codex Vaticanus: ypsistou (ΥΨΙϹΤΟΥ). Translation: highest

• Codex Monacensis (VL 130): dei. Translation: god

• Codex Sangermanensis 4 (VL 7 : sanctificationis. Translation: sanctification

• Codex Bobbiensis (VL 135): sanctimonii. Translation: virtuousness

The temple in Jerusalem was commonly called the Temple of God, or occasionally, in some older Aramaic texts, Temple of the gods. It was rarely called the Temple of the Highest, which supports the Vaticanus version being redaction, but does not identify the era of the redaction. Early-Jewish texts from the Persian era did use the term Highest frequently, however, the Essenes also used the term, and the Tobian Jews most-likely would have had more contact with them than the Sadducees or Pharisees. Additionally, the early Aramaic-speaking Christians also used the term, so even Theodotion, who was Jewish, may have made the edit as late as circa 150 AD.

8 This final statement indicates that the original text must have been written before the first temple in Jerusalem was destroyed, in 586 BC.

9 The codices tell essentially the same story, however, the Codex Vaticanus version appears to be a Jewish redaction of the Codex Sinaiticus version. The setting of the event is during the life of Jeroboam II, the king of Samaria between circa 768 and 746 BC. His kingdom briefly conquered the Arameans of Damascus and Hama, creating the largest Israelite kingdom since the era of King David, and the largest that is known archaeologically, as evidence of the earlier United Kingdom of Israel has yet to be found. He was recorded as building shrines with icons of the calf-god in them, which outraged the prophets at the time, including Amos.

The Vaticanus's version of the verse in shorter, referring to the Ba'al calf, which is anachronistic, as the god Ba'al Hadad was not depicted as a calf, although he was depicted as having horns, like many Middle-eastern gods. Based on the archaeological evidence, such as the potshards discovered at Khirbet el-Kom and Kuntillet Ajrud, the calf-god worshiped in Samaria circa 800 BC was Yahweh. The Sinaiticus version does not name the calf, however, does mention the town of Dan, which was where Jeroboam II built a shrine to the calf-god.

10 Codex Sinaiticus: prosêlytoes (ΠΡΟCΗΛΥΤΟΙC)

The Septuagint uses prosêlytoes (προσηλύτοις) in places where the Masoretic Texts has ger (גֵּר), meaning stranger, foreigner, or alien. It is generally accepted that this term referred to any foreigner that had converted to the Israelite religion(s), however, Tobit's inclusion of them in this verse implies they were seen as destitute within Israelite society at the time.

11 Greek: Midian (ΜΗΔΙΑΝ)

Media was the name of the land of the Medes, and ancient Iranian people who lived in northern Iran before the rise of the Persian Empire. The Medians were the allies of the Babylonians that jointly conquered the Assyrian Empire, a few decades after the story is set.

12 Codex Sinaiticus: Sennachirim (CΕΝΝΑΧΗΡΙΜ)

• Codex Venetus (LXX V): Chirim (ΧΕΙΡΕΙΜ)

- LXX 74: Rim (Ⲣιμ)

- LXX 314: Chirim (ⲭιⲣιμ)

- LXX 98: Senachrim (Ⲥⲉⲛⲁⲭⲣιμ)

- LXX 318: Senachirim (Ⲥⲉⲛⲁⲭιⲣιμ)

- LXX 106: Senachirim (Ⲥⲉⲛⲁⲭιⲣιμ)

- LXX 130: Senachrim (Ⲥⲉⲛⲁⲭⲣιμ)

- LXX 71: Senachirim (Ⲥⲉⲛⲁⲭιⲣιμ)

- LXX 76: Senachirim (Ⲥⲉⲛⲁⲭιⲣιμ)

- LXX 402: Senacherim (Ⲥⲉⲛⲁⲭⲉⲣιμ)

- LXX 126: Senachechrim (Ⲥⲉⲛⲁⲭⲉⲭⲣιμ)

- LXX 319: Senachri (Ⲥⲉⲛⲁⲭⲣι)

- LXX 46: Sennachrib (Ⲥⲉⲛⲛⲁⲭⲣιⲃ)

- LXX 44: Naxim (Ⲛⲁⲭιμ)

- Sahidic manuscripts: Senakherim (Ⲥⲉⲛⲁⲭⲉⲣιⲙ)

King Sennacherib was the king of the Assyrian Empire between 705 and 681 BC. His reign was spent fighting a series of insurrections in Babylonia and Canaan. He also launched a punitive invasion of Elam, that virtually wiped out the nation. His campaigns in Canaan included laying siege to Jerusalem, which had previously been allied to Assyria.

13 Codex Sinaiticus: basileus tou ouranou (ʙᴀcιᴧᴇʏcᴛoʏ oʏᴘᴀɴoʏ). Translation: king the vaulted-sky

- Codex Sangermanensis 4 (VL 7 : deus. Translation: god

- Codex Monacensis (VL 130): dominus. Translation: lord

While this term can be interpreted as references to several gods in the region, the one most-likely intended was Ashur (✳╟╫⚏◻︎), who under Sargon II's rule became known as Anshar (↦╂◁) meaning the 'whole sky.' Ashur was the king of the gods in the Assyrian pantheon since the mid-3rd-millennium BC, however, during Sargon II's rule also became a sky-god.

14 This was the year 681 BC, when Sennacherib was killed by his sons Arda-Mulissu and Nabu-shar-usur. This is calculated by Assyriologists as having taken place on 20 October, meaning Tobit would have gone into hiding sometime in mid-September. The Codex Vaticanus reads 'less than 50 days.'

15 Codex Sinaiticus: Ararat (ᴀᴘᴀᴘᴀᴛ)

- Codex Vaticanus: Ararath (ᴀᴘᴀᴘᴀⴱ)

- Sahidic manuscripts: Ararad (ⲁⲣⲁⲣⲁⲇ)

The Assyrian records record the princes as retreating to the Kingdom of ^{kur}Urartu (𒆳𒌑𒀭) in the Armenian Highlands. The name of this country was recorded as Ararat (אֲרָרָט) in Hebrew, and Urartu (Ուրարտու) in Armenian. The Greek name is a transliteration of the Hebrew name, however, the more common historical name of Urartu is used in this translation.

16 Codex Sinaiticus: Sacherdonos (ϲⲁⲭⲉⲣⲇⲟⲛⲟϲ)

* Codex Alexandrinus: Sacherdan (ϲⲁⲭⲉⲣⲇⲁⲛ)

* Codex Venetus: Nacherdonos (ⲛⲁⲭⲉⲣⲇⲟⲛⲟϲ)

* LXX 74: Sacherdônos (ϲⲁⲭⲟϥⲇⲱⲟⲛⲟϲ)

* LXX 314: Sacherdon (ϲⲁⲭⲟϥⲇⲱⲟⲛ)

* LXX 538: Sacherdôn (ϲⲁⲭⲟϥⲇⲱⲟⲛ)

* LXX 64: Sarchedonos (ϲⲁϥⲭⲟⲇⲟⲛⲟⲥ)

* LXX 46: Sachedôr (ϲⲁⲭⲟⲇⲱⲟϥ)

* LXX 248: Acherdonos (ⲁⲭⲟϥⲇⲟⲛⲟϲ)

* LXX 98: Achirdônos (ⲁⲭⲟⲓϥⲇⲱⲟⲛⲟϲ)

* LXX 542: Nachordanos (ⲛⲁⲭⲟϥⲇⲁⲇⲛⲟϲ)

* Sahidic manuscripts: Sakherdônias (ⲥⲁⲭⲉⲣⲇⲱⲛⲓⲁⲥ)

* Armenian Bible: Asordan (Ասորդւան)

* Codex Codex Corbeiensis (VL 150): Archedonassar

* Codex Monacensis (VL 130): Arcedonossar

* Codex Bobbiensis (VL 135): Nachoda

- Codex Complutensis 1 (VL 109): Natordan

Esarhaddon is the more common name of King Aššur-Aḫa-Iddina, Sennacherib's youngest son and heir. The name Esarhaddon is derived from the Latin Hazor Haddan, which was in turn derived from the Greek Asarchaddon (Ασαρχαδδων), which was used in direct translations from Assyrian texts. Sacherdonos (Σαχερδονος) appears to be a Greek transliteration of the Aramaic version of his name.

17 Codex Sinaiticus: Achicharon (ⲀⲬⲒⲬⲀⲢⲞⲚ)

- Codex Vaticanus: Achiacharon (ⲀⲬⲒⲀⲬⲀⲢⲞⲚ)

- LXX 107: Achiachar (ⲀⲬⲒⲀⲬⲀⲢ)

- Vetus Latina manuscripts: Achicarum

This name is generally translated as Ahikar, the famous, possibly fictional hero of the Words of Ahikar, the oldest known Jewish or Samaritan text to survive intact to the present. The oldest copy found to date is from around 500 BC, a couple of centuries older than the oldest of the Dead Sea Scrolls. Tobit does allude to the story of Ahikar's betrayal by his nephew, which is found in the Words of Ahikar, and it is accepted that this was a reference to that Ahikar, however, both stories are also regarded as fiction by most scholars, and so the authors may have been the same person.

It is also possible that both books began as historical texts that then became fictionalized, however, if additional elements were added, they must have been added to the Words of

Ahikar before the oldest surviving copy, from circa 500 BC. As both Ahikar and Tobit are reported to have lived circa 700 BC, this is not a great deal of time for the books to have been altered, however, as all books were copied by hand at the time, it is possible that the scribes felt a more fantastic version of the tales of these two men's lives would sell better.

Tobit (Sinaiticus): Chapter 2

King Esarhaddon restored to me my home, and this afforded my wife Hannah, and my son Tobiah to prepare a Pentecost feast, which is the holy feast of the seven weeks, there was a good breakfast prepared for me, in which I sat down to eat., and he sat next to me at the table

When I sat down and saw the abundance of fish on the table, I said to Tobiah my son, "Child, walk around and look for an indigent brother who is captive in Nineveh, who remembers God[1] in his heart, and bring him to eat with me. I'll wait for you to return."

Then Tobiah went out to look for an indigent brother of ours, but when he returned he called out, "Father."

I answered, "Here I am."

He stated, "Father, one of our nation is murdered, and is throw down in the marketplace, and is laying there right now!"

Then I jumped to leave before I had tasted any of it, and retrieved him from the square and placed him in a shed until the sun sank, and then I buried him. Then I returned, and bathed myself, and ate my food after morning, remembering the words of the prophet of Amos[2] who said in Bethel, "Your feasts will be turned into mourning, and all your songs into lamentations." I wept, and after the sunset, I went and dug a grave and buried him.

Those near me laughed at me, saying, "He's not afraid any longer. Already he has been searched for to be executed for this thing and ran away, and again he buries their dead."

The same night I returned from bathing, I entered my courtyard to sleep, and despite the walls of my courtyard, my face was uncovered because of the heat. I did not know that there were sparrows inside with me, and while I was gazing up, they defecated into my eyes, causing a warm white film. I went to the physicians to be cured, but after many ointments and many medicines, I was still going blind, and my eyes continued to have white film until I was quite blind, and I was weak and without eyes for four years.

All of my brothers grieved for me, and Ahikar supported me for two years before he went to Elam.[3] Eventually Hannah, my wife, took inside work with women.

Once when the lord of the place paid her, he gave the salary on the seventh of Dystrus,[4] when she took down the loom beam,[5] the lord sent her off with her regular wages and also gave her a goat kid for the house. When she returned with the kid, the first time it bleated, I called her and I asked, "Where did this kid come from. Did you steal it? Return it quickly as the lord is powerful, and we have never eaten anything stolen."

She replied to me, "It was given as a gift in addition to my wages."

I did not believe her and commanded her to return it to its owner, and I was angry because of it, but she replied to me, "What about your charitable works and your just deeds? All your works are known!"

Tobit (Sinaiticus): Chapter 2 Notes

1 Codex Sinaiticus: êlê (ΗλΗ)

• Codex Vaticanus: cyriou (ΚΥΡΙΟΥ). Translation: lord (main, chief, dominant, master)

The Sinaiticus version of Tobit includes a direct Greek transliteration of the Aramaic elah (ﬡﬥﬣ) meaning 'god,' which proves the translators were working off of an Aramaic source-text.

2 The prophet Amos was active in Samaria and Judah between 760 and 755 BC, and is believed to have died in 745 BC, about 66 years before this event.

3 Codex Sinaiticus: Elymaeda (ЄλΥΜλιΔλ)

• Codex Vaticanus: Ellymaeda (ЄλλΥΜλιΔλ)

• LXX 107: Elimaeda (Єλιμλιλλ)

• LXX 98: Eloemaeda (Ελοιμαιδα)

• LXX 71: Elemaeda (ЄλϬμλιλλ)

• LXX 126: Lymaeda (λυμλιλλ)

• Codex Corbeiensis (VL 150): Limaidam

• Codex Monacensis (VL 130): Lymaidem

Haltamti (𒁹𒄠𒋾𒆠𒉈) was a major nation in southern modern Iran, until it was virtually destroyed by the kings of Assyria in the 7th century BC. The Babylonian name of the land was Elamma[ki] (𒌷𒉏𒆠), which was adopted into

Hebrew as Eilam (עֵילָם) and Greek as Elám (Ἐλάμ), ultimately resulting in the modern English name Elam. The conflict in question is likely the events near the beginning of Esarhaddon's rule, when an ethnically Elamite Assyrian governor named Nabu-zer-kitti-lišir in southern Babylonia revolted against Assyrian rule and besieged Ur. Esarhaddon's army defeated Nabu-zer-kitti-lišir, and he fled to Elam, where he was ultimately captured and executed.

4 Codex Sinaiticus: Dystrou (ⲇⲩⲥⲧⲣⲟⲩ). Translation: Dystrus

Dystrus was the fifth month of the ancient Macedonian calendar, and then the corresponding month in the Seleucid calendar, developed after General Seleucus I Nicator's reconquest of Babylon in 312 BC. The Seleucid calendar was in use for centuries in the Middle East, well into the Christian Era in some regions, however, was never in use in Egypt, where the Ptolemy's adopted the Egyptian Civil Calendar, and renamed the months to correspond with the Athenian calendar. This indicates that the Sinaiticus version of Tobit was not translated in Alexandria, but somewhere in the Seleucid Empire, which included most of the territory of modern Iran, Iraq, Syria, Lebanon. Afghanistan, Turkmenistan, Pakistan, Uzbekistan, and Turkey, at their height. It is likely that it was adopted by the editor of the Codex Sinaiticus as it appears to be an older and superior copy of Tobit, nevertheless, almost certainly not the translation made in Alexandria.

5 Codex Sinaiticus: istos (ιϲτοϲ). Translation: mast (or shinbone, beam or a loom, loom, web of a loom)

Unlike the modern loom, in the ancient Greek looms had upright beams.

Tobit (Sinaiticus): Chapter 3

I became depressed and sighed, and cried, and after sighing, I prayed, "Sydyk exists![1] Lord, all your works are fair, and all your ways are mercy and truth, and you judge truly and justly for ages. Now, remember me, and look down on me. Don't punish me for my sins and ignorance, and the sins of my fathers, who have sinned before you, and did not obey your commandments, and broke your covenant with us, therefore you have given us as captives, and to death, and as a parable of humbleness and an insult before all the nations among whom we are scattered. Now, your judgments are many and true. Deal with me according to my sins and my forefathers' because we have not kept your commandments, nor have walked in truth before you.

Now, if it is acceptable to you take my spirit from me, and remove me from the face of the Earth, and make me dirt rather than life, as I am insulted and lied to, and have many regrets. Lord, command that I may be released from my duties, and taken to the place of ages. Don't turn your face away from me."

On the day this happened, Sarah the daughter of Raguel in the city of Ecbatana[2] in Media, overheard an insult from a child, and a reproach against her father, because she was given to husbands seven times, and

Asmodeus[3] the cunning demon[4] had killed them before she was with them in the way of women.

Then the children said, "You have killed your man! Already you were given seven husbands, and you were not called by any of their names. Why do you whip us because of these men? If they are dead, go be with them, and let us not see either a son or daughter from you for ages."

On that day, she was depressed in the mind, and cried, and got up and went upstairs and was considering hanging herself, but reconsidered, and said, "I could never do this to my father. If a family exists and their only daughter hanged herself, it will be a reproach, and I will bring his old age with sadness to Hades.[5] It would be better if I was not strangled, but I lack a husband, and therefore am insulted and mocked all my life."

At that time she held her hands up to the window, and said, "Bless you God, and blessed is your name for ages. Let all praise you forever, and your projects in their ages. Now, I turn I my face and my eyes and look up and say, 'Take me out of the earth, that I may no longer hear the reproach.' You know, Lord,[6] that I am pure from all sin with a man, and that I never defiled my name, or the name of my father, in the land of my captivity. I am the only daughter of my father, and he has no other child to be his heir, nor a brother, nor any near relative to whom I may offer myself to as a wife. My seven husbands are already dead, and why do I exist? I don't expect to have a family, and should die, Lord, now, hear my insults."

At that time, both prayers were heard before the glory of God, and he sent Raphael[7] to heal the two, to Tobit to destroy the white film from his eyes, so that he may perceive with his eyes the light of God, and to Sarah, for Raphael to give to her Tobiah the son of Tobit as a wife, and to drive Asmodeus the cunning demon from her, because she belonged to Tobiah by right of inheritance. Tobit returned into his house from of court-yard, and Sarah of Raguel descended from the upper floor.

Tobit (Sinaiticus): Chapter 3 Notes

1 Codex Sinaiticus: Dicaeos i (ⲇⲓⲕⲁⲓⲟⲥⲉⲓ). Translation: Justice exists, fairness exists

The name Dicaeos (Δίκαιος) was repeatedly used in the books of prophecy of the Septuagint were the word ṣdq (צדק) is used in the Masoretic Texts. Both words translate as 'justice' or 'fairness,' however, the term was also the name of the Canaanite and early-Israelite god of Justice, Sydyk, which also became the Hebrew name of the Roman god Jupiter, and continues to be the Hebrew name for the planet Jupiter. As this is a statement at the beginning of a prayer, 'Dicaeos exists,' it seems more likely that Tobit was addressing the then-popular Israelite god Sydyk, than making a generic declaration, and so 'Sydyk exists' is used in this translation. In the Greek era, Sydyk was worshiped by the Hassidian sect of Judahites, who migrated to northern Italy and Dalmatia during the Maccabean Revolt.

2 Codex Sinaiticus: Ekbatanois (ⲉⲕⲃⲁⲧⲁⲛⲟⲓⲥ)

- LXX 243: Ecbasanoes (ⲈⳐⲩⲗⲟⲥⲇⲫⲟⲓⲥ)

- Codex Complutensis 1 (VL 109): Bethanis

- Ge'ez manuscripts: Biṭani (ቢጣኒ)

Ecbatana was the capital of the Median Empire, and later the summer capital of the Persian Empire. Its name translates in old Persian as 'the place of gathering.'

3 Codex Sinaiticus: Asmodeos (ΑϹΜΟΔΕΟϹ)

- Codex Vaticanus: Asmodaus (ΑϹΜΟΔΑΥϹ)
- LXX 319: Asmodeus (Ασμοδέυϲ)
- LXX 46: Asmodaeon (Ασμοδαιον)
- Codex Bobbiensis (VL 135): Asmadeum
- Codex Complutensis 1 (VL 109): Nasbodeus

Asmodeus is a Jewish and Samaritan demon, adopted from the Zoroastrian faith. The name is derived from the Avestan aēšəma daēuua (𐬀𐬉𐬱𐬆𐬨𐬀 𐬛𐬀𐬉𐬎𐬎𐬀), which translates as wrath-demon. At the time, Zoroastrianism was one of the religions practiced in Media.

4 Codex Sinaiticus: to daemonion to ponêron (ΤΟ ΔΑΙΜΟΝΙΟΝ ΤΟ ΠΟΝΗΡΟΝ). Translation: the demon (or divine, lesser god, powerful spirit) the wrathful (or painful, oppressive, grievous)

- Codex Vaticanus: to ponêron daemonion (ΤΟΠΟΝΗΡΟΝ ΔΑΙΜΟΝΙΟΝ). Translation: the wrathful (or painful, oppressive, grievous) demon (or divine, lesser god, powerful spirit)

The Greek term has many interpretations, and at its core relates to something powerful. As the being in question was a Zoroastrian demon, the original term used in the Aramaic text was likely and Aramaic translation of the Avestan term aēšəma daēuua (ܐܫܡܕܐܐ ܘ ܕܐܘܘܐ), which translates as 'wrath demon.'

5 Codex Sinaiticus: aidou (ΑΙΔΟΥ). Translation: Hades

6 Codex Sinaiticus: despota (ΔΕϹΠΟΤΑ). Translation: despot (or tyrant, lord, bishop, master, ruler)

• Codex Vaticanus: cyrie (ΚΥΡΙΕ). Translation: lord (or main, chief, dominant, master)

As both despota and cyrie are used in the Septuagint as translations of a word meaning Lord, it is unlikely that either of the two codices was based on the other, as there would have been no reason to replace one word with the other. This points to two separate translations of the Book of Tobit into Greek from Aramaic.

7 Codex Sinaiticus: Rafail (ΡΑΦΑΗΛ)

• Codex Vaticanus: megalou Raphaêl (ΜΕΓΑΛΟΥ ΡΑΦΑΗΛ). Translation: great Raphael

• LXX 126: megalou Theos cae apestile Cyrios Raphaêl ton angelon autou (μόγαλου Θόος ἱλι ἀπόστόιλό Κυβιος Ραφαλλ τον ἀγγόλον ἀυτου). Translation: great god and sent Lord Raphael the messenger himself

• LXX 311: megalou apestal Raphaêl (μόγαλου ἀπόσταλ Ραφαλλ). Translation: great apostle Raphael

• Codex Bobbiensis (VL 135): Raphael angelus. Translation: Raphael angel

Raphael was a messenger in some Jewish sects and later adopted by Christians and Muslims. Raphael only appears in the books of Tobit and Enoch (1st Enoch). Both seem to have been important to the Essen community later, and neither was of interest to the Pharisees or Sadducees. As Josephus claimed the Essenes considered themselves to be descents of the ancient Canaanites, it is plausible that this name started as a reference to the healing god (Rapha El), who was worshiped in Canaan before the Israelites conquered the Canaanites.

Tobit (Sinaiticus): Chapter 4

On that day, Tobit remembered the silver that he had loaned to Gabael in Ray[1] in Media, and said in his heart, "I have wished for death, no! I will call for my son Tobiah, so I can tell him about the silver before I die."

He called Tobiah his son, and when he came to his side, he said, "Bury me honorably, and support your mother, and don't abandon her all the days of your life, and do that which is acceptable to her, and do not grieve her spirit ever. Remember, my son, that she saw many dangers for you when you were in her womb, and when she is dead, bury her next to me in the same grave."

"My son, be mindful of our Lord all your days and don't let your will be set to sin or to transgress his commandments. Do correctly all your life, and don't follow the ways of dishonesty. If you deal honestly, your business will prosper and you will succeed. Give to charities from your property. The Lord gives to those that follow the noble counsel and the will of the Lord. Now, child, I signify for our family, that I placed ten talents of silver with Gabael, the son of Gabri in Ray in Media."

Don't be afraid, my son, that we are made poor, for you have much honest wealth, if you fear God, and flee from all sin, and do that which is pleasing in the sight of Lord your god.

Tobit (Sinaiticus): Chapter 4 Notes

1 Codex Sinaiticus: Argoes (ⲁⲣⲅⲟⲓⲥ)

- Codex Vaticanus: Ragoes (ⲣⲁⲅⲟⲓⲥ)
- LXX 318: Ragoê (ⲣⲁⲅⲟⲏ)
- LXX 670: Raga (ⲣⲁⲅⲁ)
- LXX 319: Rassois (ⲣⲁⲥⲥⲟⲓⲥ)
- LXX 64: Agrois (ⲁⲅⲣⲟⲓⲥ)

This is accepted as the Greek name of Ray (ری), an ancient city near Tehran in Iran. It is regarded as the oldest continuously inhabited city in Tehran Province, dating back to the Median Empire. The Greek name used in this book is likely a transliteration of the Aramaic name of the era, itself transliterated from the Assyrian name Raga ([illegible]). The older Elamite name was Rakkaan ([illegible]), while the later Old Persian name was Ragae (𐎼𐎥𐎠).

Tobit (Sinaiticus): Chapter 5

Then Tobiah answered Tobit his father, "Everything, you have told me I will do, father. But how can I receive the silver, seeing I do not know him? What token can he see and believe me and give me the silver? Also, I don't know the roads of Media to travel there."

Then Tobit responded and said to Tobiah his son, "This is the document he gave me, a handwritten agreement made between the two of us. Each took a copy, when I left the silver there, more than twenty years ago,[1] so request the silver. And now, child, find a trustworthy man who will travel with you, and pay him to travel to the east, and carry the silver."

Tobiah went out to search for a man to travel with him to Media who knew the roads, and while he was out happened upon Raphael the messenger,[2] standing across from him, and he did not know that he was a messenger of God, and he asked him, "Who are you, young man?"

He asked him, "From the Israelites, your brothers. I came here looking for work."

He asked him, "Do you know the roads that go to Media?"

He answered, "Yes, I have traveled there often, and am experienced and knowledgeable of all the roads. Also,

I have traveled in Media and lodged near Gabael our brother's house in Ray in Media, and it is only two days travel along the road from Ecbatana to Ray and lies in the mountains."

He asked, "Wait for me, young man, until I go to get my father's advice, since I need someone to travel with me, and my family will pay you."

He replied to him, "I'll wait, only don't take long."

Tobiah went to tell Tobit his father, and said, "I found a man from among our brothers, the Israelites."

He replied, "Call this man to me, so I may know of what tribe he is, and whether he is a trustworthy man to travel with you, child."

So Tobiah went and called him, saying, "Young man, my father calls you in."

He went to him, and spoke with Tobit, saying, "Amen[3] bring you much joy!"

Tobit replied to him, "What do I have to be happy about? I am a feeble man, blind, and unable to see the light of the sky,[4] but I stand in the shadow of death, to be mocked by the light. I am the living dead. I hear the voice of men, but I cannot see them."

He replied, "Have courage, God may heal you. Have courage."

Tobit replied to him, "Tobiah my son wants to travel to Media. If you are capable of traveling with him leading him, my family will pay you, brother."

He replied, "I am capable of traveling with him. I am knowledgeable of all the roads, and have often gone to Media, passing through the fields and the mountains. I know all the roads.

He asked him, "Brother, who is your father, and which tribe are you from? Tell me, brother."

He answered, "What do you need a tribe for?"

He said to him, I want to know truthfully, who are you brother, and what is your name?"

He answered him, "I am Azariah of the great Hananiah, your brother."

He replied, "Greetings and welcome, brother. Don't be angry brother, because I demanded to know the truth of who your father was, and you, child, are from a good and noble family. I know Hananiah and Nathan,[5] the two sons of the great Shemaiah and they accompanied me in Jerusalem, and they worshiped with me there, and they did not sin. Your brothers are good and your people are good, your are from a good root. Come and celebrate."

And he offered, "I will pay you a beka[6] each day, and costs equal to my son's, and you will travel with my son, and also my family will add a bonus."

He replied, "I will travel with him and don't be afraid, he will be safe departing, and safely returned to you because the roads are safe."

He said to him, "Amen bless you, brother," and he said to his son, "Child, prepare for the road, and leave with this brother, and the god in the sky[7] will protect you on the way there and return you to me safely, and his messenger accompanying you will protect you, child."

As he set out on the road and said goodbye to his father and his mother, Tobit said, "Travel safely."

His mother wept and said to Tobit "Why have you sent away my child? Is he not the staff of our hand, going in and out before us? Do not be greedy to add silver to silver, but let it be considered as nothing in comparison to our child, Amen! For that which the Lord has given us to live with is enough for us."

He replied to her, "Don't worry, he will travel safely, and safely return to us, and your eyes will see him in the future when he returns safely. There is no reason to be fearful about it sister, as the good messenger will keep him company, and his journey will be prosperous, and he will return safe," and so she stopped crying.

Tobit (Sinaiticus): Chapter 5 Notes

1 This reference to twenty years is consistent with Tobit's claims to have traveled to Media for King Sargon II (Ενεμεσσαρου), and to be sending his son there again during the time of King Esarhaddon (Σαχερδονος). Sargon II ruled between 722 and 705 BC, and Esarhaddon ruled between 681 and 669 BC. If the roads were closed during at least some of the reign of Sennacherib (Σενναχηριμ), as previously stated, then that would have been between 705 and 681 BC, a time period of 24 years.

Most of Sennacherib's reign was focused on suppressing local rebellions, including a major rebellion in Babylonia backed by Elam. It is unclear what the situation was with Media at the time as there are few records, however, Media did back the later Babylonian rebellion that toppled the Assyrian Empire in 612 BC, and so it is plausible they had backed the Babylonian rebellion in 689 BC as well.

2 Codex Sinaiticus: angelos tou theou (ⲀⲅⲅⲉⲗⲟⲥⲦⲞⲨ ⲐⲈⲞⲨ). Translation: messenger of the god

• Codex Vaticanus: angelos (Ⲁⲅⲅⲉⲗⲟⲥ). Translation: messenger

• LXX 236: angelon (ἀγγόλον). Translation: messenger

• LXX 71: angelos Cyriou (ἀγγόλος Κυρίου). Translation: messenger of Lord

3 Codex Sinaiticus: Genoeto (ΓЄΝΟΙΤΟ)

- LXX 71: Genêtae (Γ ϬΝΙͭΤΑΙ)

The Greek term Genoeto (Γένοιτο) is used in the Septuagint as a translation of the word that is represented in the Masoretic texts as Amen (אָמֵן), and therefore restored in this translation, however, in the Codex Sinaiticus' version of Tobit, it is used as a proper name, and in chapter 10 it is referred to as God's great name, suggesting that the Samaritans viewed Amen the Egyptian sun-god as another version of Shemesh, the Israelite sun-god prior to King Josiah's banning the worship of Shemesh circa 625 BC.

4 Codex Sinaiticus: ouranou (ΟΥΡΑΝΟΥ). Translation: vaulted-sky

As the original term was in Aramaic, but it is unclear whether it was Shamayim or Bethel, the generic translation of 'sky' is used.

5 Codex Sinaiticus: Nathan (ΝΑΘΑΝ)

- Codex Vaticanus: Iathan (ΙΑΘΑΝ)

- LXX 319: Nathanian (Ναθανιαν)

- Codex Sangermanensis 4: Athaniam

Iathan is almost certainly a misspelling of Nathan, as it is only known from the books of Tobit. This suggests that even though the Sinaiticus Codex version of Tobit has many of what appear to be spelling errors in the Greek text if one assumes a Koine origin, the text was copied correctly by the scribes. The Sinaiticus text contains many words that were more common in the Ionic dialect than the Attic, which was the ancestral-dialect of Koine, suggesting that the errors may have simply been Ionic spelling variation.

6 Codex Sinaiticus: drachmên (ⲆⲢⲀⲬⲘⲎⲚ)

• Codex Corbeiensis (VL 150): didragmam

The drachma was a Greek coin used from around 1100 BC, worth approximately 4.3 grams of silver. The name drachma was used in the Septuagint as a translation for the beka (בֶּקַע), was the half-shekel measurement used in ancient Canaan. As 'drachma' was the Greek translation of beka, the term beka is restored.

7 Codex Sinaiticus: theos o en tô ouranô (ⲐⲈⲞⲤⲞⲈⲚⲦⲰ ⲞⲨⲢⲀⲚⲰ). Translation: god that is the Uranus (or sky)

• Codex Vaticanus: ouranô oecôn theos (ⲞⲨⲢⲀⲚⲰⲞⲒⲔⲰⲚ ⲐⲈⲞⲤ). Translation: Uranus (or sky) house god

The proper name of Uranus is used in both versions, however, could not have been in the Aramaic source text the Greeks used. The name is found in both versions of Tobit, and so it is likely that it was in the original Greek translations. The Vaticanus version clearly points to the Aramaic source as referring to Bytâl (ⲤⲚⲠⲀⳞ), the Canaanite and early-Israelite sky-god, however, the Sinaiticus is more generic in its translation of the source.

According to both the prophet Jeremiah, who was present for the destruction of Jerusalem, and settled with the Israelite refugees in southern Egypt, as well as the archaeological evidence in southern Egypt, the Israelite refugees continued worshiping Bytål, along with Yahw and Anat until at least the Persian era. Nevertheless, this manuscript is not clear on which sky-god is being addressed, possibly because the Greeks had just conquered the Persians, and Alexander was in the process of exterminating the Zoroastrian magi, and the translator wanted the Greek reader of the text to infer the god in the sky was Zeus. In any event, the god in question was likely Bytål/Bethel/Baitylos or Shamayim/Anu, as these gods were widely worshiped by the Samaritans before King Jeroboam II decided everyone should worship the calf-god Yahweh, which Tobit had rejected.

Tobit (Sinaiticus): Chapter 6

They traveled, the young man and the messenger with him, and his dog also walked alongside him. They traveled together until one night when they camped along the bank of the Tigris River. The young man went down to wash his feet in the Tigris River, and a huge fish came out of the water intending to bite off the foot of the young man, but the messenger called out to the young man, "Avoid the fish, and catch it!"

The young man was strong and dragged the fish up onto the land, and the messenger stated, "Cut up the fish, and remove the bile, and the heart, and the liver, and keep the guts on yourself. There are useful medicines[1] that can be made from the bile, and the heart and the liver, but cook the fish eat it, and salt the rest to eat on the road."

Then they continued traveling together on the road to Ecbatana, and the young man asked the messenger, "Azariah, brother, what medicine is made from the heart and the liver and the bile of the fish?"

He answered him, "The heart and the liver of the fish can be smoked in front of a man or woman who is possessed with a demon or destructive spirit,[2] and it will leave its possessee, and not return to him for ages, and the bile can be used to anoint the eyes of a man with white film formed on them, and the white film will be healed."

When they had crossed into Media and were approaching Ecbatana, Raphael said to Tobiah, the young man, "Brother."

He replied, "I'm here."

He stated, "We will lodge with Raguel tonight, who is your male relative and has a daughter named Sarah, and no other son or daughter exists other than Sarah alone. You are her kin and so you can inherit everything through her. The claim through her father's family justifies the inheritance, and the girl is wise and courageous, and very good, and her father is good."

He continued, "It is justified you take her. Hear me, brother, and speak to her father about the girl tonight, so that you may take her as your bride when you return from Ray, and can be wed to her, and know that Raguel will not refuse you from being married, without incurring death by going against the judgment of the book of Moses. Know that you will inherit, if you take his daughter, before all other people. Now, listen to me brother, and talk about the girl tonight, and make an agreement with the family, so when you return from Ray, we may take her back to your home."

Then Tobiah replied to Raphael, "Azariah, brother, I heard that she has already been given to seven men, who died in the bride-chamber[3] the night of their marriage to her. They are now dead, and I heard it said that a demon killed them, and now I'm afraid, not of her injustice, but of that who wishes to be with her, it may murder me. I am my father's only child, and I am afraid, I will die, and bring my father's and my mother's life to the grave with sorrow because of me, for they have no other son to bury them."

Then he replied to him, "Don't you remember the commands which your father gave you, that you should marry a wife of your own family? Now, listen to me, brother, and don't be concerned about the demon but marry her, and know that tonight she will be given you in marriage. When you enter the bride-chamber, take the liver of the fish, and its heart and add them to the ashes on the incense burners, and a strong odor will emerge, and when the demon smells it will flee and not bother her again forever."

Tobit (Sinaiticus): Chapter 6 Notes

1 Codex Sinaiticus: pharmacon (ⲪⲀⲢⲘⲀⲔⲞⲚ). Translation: medicine (or drug, potion, remedy)

• LXX 319: pharmaca (ⲪⲀⲢⲘⲀⲕⲀ). Translation: medicine (or drug, potion, poison)

• Codex Complutensis 1 (VL 109): medicamenta. Translation: medicines (or drugs, remedies)

2 Codex Sinaiticus: daimoniou ê pneumatos ponêrou (ⲆⲀⲒⲘⲞⲚⲒⲞⲨ Ⲏ ⲠⲚⲈⲨⲘⲀⲦⲞⲤ ⲠⲞⲚⲎⲢⲞⲨ). Translation: demon (or lesser god, powerful spirit, divinity) or (or as) spirit (or wind, breath, life, air, angel) destructive (or painful, grievous)

• Codex Vaticanus: daemonion ê paneuma ponêron (ⲆⲀⲒⲘⲞⲚⲒⲞⲚ Ⲏ ⲠⲀⲚⲈⲨⲘⲀ ⲠⲞⲚⲎⲢⲞⲚ). Translation: demon (or lesser god, powerful spirit, divinity) or (or as) spirit (or wind, breath, life, air, angel) destructive (or painful, grievous)

• LXX 71: daemonion (ⲆⲀⲒⲙⲟⲚⲒⲟⲚ). Translation: demon (or lesser god, powerful spirit, divinity)

The phrase appears to originate in the Zoroastrian terms daeva (و_سیﺟو), meaning 'demon,' and Angra Mainyu (سۆﻮﺟﻰﺳ), meaning 'destructive spirit.'

3 Codex Sinaiticus: nymphôn (ⲚⲨⲘⲫⲱⲚ). Translation: nuptial apartment

- LXX 319: nymphôni (ⲛⲩⲙⲫⲟⲟⲛⲓ). Translation: nuptial apartment

- Codex Complutensis 1 (VL 109): nuptias. Translation: weddings

The Greek word nymphôn (νυμφων) referred to a room in which marriages were consummated, much like a modern honeymoon suit, although more formal.

Tobit (Sinaiticus): Chapter 7

When they arrived in Ecbatana, he stated, "Azariah, brother, lead me straight to Raguel our brother," and he led him to Raguel's house, and they found him sitting at the door to his courtyard.

He welcomed them, saying, "Greetings brothers," and welcomed them into his house.

Edna, his wife asked, "How much does this young man look like my cousin Tobit!" and then Edna asked them, "From where are you, brothers?"

They answered, "We are of the Naphtalites who were taken captives to Nineveh."

Then they asked them, "Do you know Tobit our relative?"

They answered, "We know him."

Then they asked, "Is he well?"

They answered, "Alive, and in good health," and Tobiah added, "he is my father."

Then Raguel leaped up, and kissed him, and wept. He said to him, "Amen bless you, child. You are of a kind and noble father! Oh, he suffers badly! That blind man, honest, but a source of great pity." He hugged Tobiah their brother around the neck and wept, and Edna his wife, and Sarah their daughter also wept. Nevertheless, they welcomed them cheerfully into their house, and they bathed and cleaned their feet.

Then make a meal, and Tobiah said to Raphael, "Azariah, brother, talk to Raguel about me and Sarah, my sister."

Raguel listened to the reasoning and said to the young man, "Eat and drink, be celebrate tonight young man, as no other man will take Sarah my daughter, except you, brother. I will not give her to any man but you, as you are my very nearest and most intimate family, child. I have engaged her to seven men, brother, and everyone died on his wedding night when led into the bride-chamber. Now, child, eat and drink, and the Lord will work through you."

Tobiah replied, "I will not eat or drink anything here until you come to an agreement with me."

Raguel said, "Agreed, Then take her from now on according to our custom, as you are her cousin, and she is yours, and the merciful God gave you good success in all things."

Then he called his daughter Sarah, and she came to her father, and he took her by the hand, and gave her to Tobiah as a wife, saying, "Look, I give her to your family according to the laws of the book of Moses, as Shamayim[1] ordered I give her to you. Take her, the sister is yours from now on brother. She is your sister, whom I give you today and for the ages, and the Lord of the sky will bless you, child, tonight, and to be fruitful as long and who have mercy and peace."

Raguel called Sarah his daughter to him, and she came, and he took her hand and gave her to him stating, "Take care of her according to our customs, and the laws written in the book of Moses, I hereby give her to you as a wife. Take her back to your father safely, and may the god Shamayim[2] bless you and give you peace."

Her mother called her and said, "Bring the book," and she wrote, 'We give her to him as a wife according to the judgments of the law of Moses,' and they began to eat and drink.

Raguel called to Edna his wife, and said, "Sister, prepare the bridal-chamber, and take them there."

She walked to the bridal-chamber and said, "Take her in," and wept with her, and said, "Be courageous daughter, the Lord Shamayim will grant you joy instead of sorrow. Be courageous daughter," and she left.

Tobit (Sinaiticus): Chapter 7 Notes

1 Codex Sinaiticus: Ouranou (ΟΥΡΑΝΟΥ). Translation: Uranus (or vaulted-sky)

In this sentence Ouranou (Οὐρανοῦ) is being used as a proper name. As this is the Greek term for both Uranus, and the vaulted-sky that covered the world in the view of most of the Classical philosophers, the Hebrew term Shamayim is used, which is both the Israelite version of Uranus: the god Shamayim (שָׁמַיִם), and the Hebrew term for the vaulted-sky. The name Shamayim was used many times in the Masoretic Texts, and his worship was banned in Judah by King Josiah circa 625 BC.

2 Codex Sinaiticus: o cyrios tou ourano (ΟΚΥΡΙΟΣΤΟΥ ΟΥΡΑΝΟ). Translation: the lord the vaulted-sky

• Codex Vaticanus: o theos tou ouranou (ΟΘΕΟΣΤΟΥ ΟΥΡΑΝΟΥ). Translation: the god the vaulted-sky

• Codex Alexandrinus: o cyrios tou ourano (ΟΘΕΟΣΤΟΥ ΟΥΡΑΝΟΤΕΚΝΑ). Translation: the god of the vaulted-sky's child (or descendant)

• LXX 107: ho cyrios Theos tou ouranou (ο μᾱϐιος Θϐος του ουϸᾱνου). Translation: the lord God of the sky

The vaulted-sky (Οὐρανοῦ) of early Greek cosmology was based on, or very similar to, the Shamayim of the ancient Canaanite and Israelite religions. The Shamayim was the first thing created in Genesis, right before Eretz (Earth).

Tobit (Sinaiticus): Chapter 8

After they had entered into the bridal-chamber, and eaten and drank, and they wanted to sleep, the young man led her into the bed room. Tobiah remembered the words of Raphael, and took the liver of the fish, and its heart from the pouch, which he was carrying, and added it to the incense ash. The odor of the fish lingered, and the demon tried to flee to the region of Egypt, but Raphael moved quickly and caught it and tied its feet together and immediately bound it in shackles, and then exited the door to the bridal-chamber.

Tobiah rose from the bed, and said, "Sister, get up, and let's pray together to our Lord to give us mercy and salvation."

They arose and began to pray in order to bring themselves salvation. They prayed, "Blessed are you, God of our fathers, and blessed is your name in all ages and generations. Praise Shamayim,[1] and your house in all ages. You created Adam and created as a helper Eve[2] his wife, and from the two of them descended all the people, and you said that it is not good that the man is alone, and you created a helper for him of his own kind. Now, I do not take my sister like a prostitute, but we come together in honesty and I will take pity on her, and we will grow old together," and he added, "Amen, amen," and they went to sleep for the night.

Raguel got up, and called the house-slave to himself, and went out and dug a grave, saying, "No one must know if he has died, or I will become the object of ridicule and insults."

They finished digging the grave and Raguel returned to the house, and called his wife and said, "Send one of the young girls, and let her see whether he is alive. If he died, we can bury him and no one will know."

She sent the young girl, who lit the lamp, and opened the door, and entered, and found them lying there passed out together. The young girl left and told them they were alive and nothing evil had happened.

They praised the god Shamayim, saying, "Blessed is God in every blessing, pure and praised in everything in the ages. It has not happened, that which I suspected, but you have dealt with us according to your great mercy. Bless and take pity on the two only-children,[3] for them to be fruitful Lord. Have mercy and give them health, and bring joy and mercy to their lives."

Then he said to his house-slave, "Be cheerful and refill the grave we dug before."

The women said, "Bake a lot of bread! Go to the cattle herd and fetch two cows and four rams," and then said, "slaughter them and begin to prepare them."

He called Tobiah and said to him, "You will remain here for fourteen days, and eat and drink with me, and be cheerful with the mind of my daughter. And half of everything that I own you will receive, and return safely to your father, and the other half will be yours when I and my wife are dead. Have courage, child, I am your father and Edna is your mother, and we are your family from now for the ages, have courage child."

Tobit (Sinaiticus): Chapter 8 Notes

1 Codex Sinaiticus: ouranoe (**OYPANOI**). Translation: skies, Uranuses

The use of the Greek translation of the word Shamayim, plural for sky, combined with the reference to his house, is a clear reference to the gods Shamayim and Bethel, who are well documented in the Masoretic Texts and archaeological records as being major Israelite gods at the time that Tobiah would have been praying.

2 Codex Sinaiticus: Evan (**EYAN**)

Evan was the Greek transliteration of Eve used in the Septuagint's book of Genesis, other than the initial reference to her as Zoe (Ζωή), meaning life.

3 Codex Sinaiticus: monogenis (**MONOΓENEIC**)

This word translates as approximately 'only member of a family,' which, strictly speaking, was not the case for Tobiah and Sarah, however, they were both the only-children of their parents, and that is likely was the Aramaic source was referring to.

Tobit (Sinaiticus): Chapter 9

Then Tobiah called Raphael, and said to him, "Azariah, brother, take with yourself four house-slaves, and two camels, and go on to Ray to visit Gabael and give him the letter, and after you have received the silver, return to the marriage. You know that my father is counting the days, and if I take even one more day, he will be very worried, however, Raguel has sworn me to stay, and I cannot leave because of the oath."

So Raphael traveled with the four house-slaves and the two camels, to Ray in Media, lodged with Gabael, and gave him the message, and told him about Tobiah, the son of Tobit, and that he took a wife, and invited him to the wedding.

And he rose counted out some seed-bags besides the amount owed and prepared everything, and they traveled together to the wedding. They entered into Raguel's and when they found Tobiah he leapt up and wept and blessed him, and said, "Noble and good man, honorable and brave, law-abiding and charitable. Lord Shamayim bless you and your wife, and the father and mother of your wife. Bless the god that saw my nephew Tobiah, who is like me."

Tobit (Sinaiticus): Chapter 10

Tobit counted day after day, and when the number of days of the journey were counted and they had not returned, then he asked, "Are they delayed, or is Gabael dead, and there is no man to give him the silver?" Then he became distressed.

Hannah his wife said, "My child is destroyed, and no longer exists, and is no longer living!" and she began to cry and sing a dirge for her son, and said, "Woe to me, children, that I sent out to walk, the light of my eyes!"

Tobit replied to her, "Calm down and think, sister. He may be safe and healthy but delayed there. The man that traveled with him is an honest brother of ours. Don't worry about him, sister. He'll return soon." He added, "Calm down, like me, and don't leap to conclusions about the death of our son, and assume without watching the road. Why grieve for our son who may return today?"

She was not convinced at all, and when the sun set sang a dirge and cry the whole night without sleeping.

When the fourteen days of the wedding had concluded, which Raguel had hosted for his daughter, Tobiah went to him and said, "I must leave. I know that my father and mother expect to see me soon. Now, I must be claiming that which my father sent me for, and must prepare to return to my family, as my father is expecting me."

Raguel replied, "Wait, child, stay with me, and I will send a messenger to Tobit your father and inform him about you."

He replied to him, "I cannot, I ask that you send me back from here to my father."

So Raguel handed over to Tobiah, Sarah his wife, and half of everything that he had, including the boy-slaves, girl-slaves, cattle, sheep, donkeys, camels, clothing, silver, and utensils. He sent them away, and sanctified them, and blessed him, saying, "Be safe, child, lead them safely. The god Shamayim will help you on the way, and Sarah your wife, and I will see your children before I die."

He said to Sarah his daughter, "Honor your parents-in-law, who are your parents now, and remain peaceful, daughter, so I may hear good things of you while I live," and bid them farewell.

Tobit (Sinaiticus): Chapter 11

When they arrived in Caserin,[1] which is near Nineveh, Raphael said, "You know, brother, how you left your father. Let's hurry ahead of your wife, and prepare the house," and so they both went ahead. He also said, "Bring the bile in your hand."

So they went their way, along with the dog.

Hannah was sitting looking down the road for her son, and when she saw him coming, she said to his father, "Look, your son comes, along with the man that went with him!"

Then Raphael said to Tobiah before they approached his father, "Know that he will open his eyes. Anoint his eyes with the bile of the fish, and they will become itchy and he will rub them, and the whiteness will fall away, and he will see you, and your father will again see the light!"

Then Hannah ran out, and fell on the neck of her son, and said to him, "Now that I have seen you, my son, I am content to die from now on!"

They both wept together. Tobit rose and put down his drink and went out the door into his courtyard, and stumbled. Tobias ran to him, and placed the bile of the fish in his eyes, and blew on the eyes, then lifted him and said, "Have courage father," and gave him the extra medicine, and pealed off the scabs from each of his eyelids with his hand.

He hugged him, and wept, and said to him, "I can see, child, with the light of my eyes!" He continued, "Bless God, and blessed his great name forever! Praise all his messengers and saints, and Amen, his great name.[2] Bless all the angels above us, in all their times, who he chastises with! I see Tobiah, my son!"

And so Tobit welcomed them with celebration, and blessed God for the restoration of his eyes, and Tobiah told his father of his success on the road. That he had recovered the silver, and that he had married Sarah, the daughter of Raguel's wife, and that she was approaching the gate to Nineveh.

Then Tobit went out to meet his daughter-in-law at the gate of Nineveh, rejoicing and praising God,

and those that saw him in Nineveh walking, and possessing all his faculties and without being led by the hand, marveled, and Tobit told those who approached him that God had pity on him and opened his eyes.

When he met Sarah the wife of Tobiah his son, he said to her, "Enter and be healthy, daughter, blessed is the god that led you to us, daughter, and blessed is your father, and blessed is Tobiah my son, and be celebrated, daughter. Enter your house in safety, celebration, and joy, enter, daughter."

It was a day of great joy for all the Judahites in Nineveh. Ahikar[3] and Nadan[4] his nephew came to celebrate the wedding of Tobiah.

Tobit (Sinaiticus): Chapter 11 Notes

1 Codex Sinaiticus: Caserin (ΚΑϹΕΡΕΙΝ)

• Codex Monacensis (VL 130): Cara

• Codex Sangermanensis 4 (VL 7 : Caracha

• Codex Complutensis 1 (VL 109): Tarram

This town is unknown to modern archaeologists, however, is likely a Greek transliteration of the Aramaic name Kashisim (ﬡﬡﬡ), itself a transliteration of the town called Kiššaššu (ﬡﬡﬡﬡ) in Assyrian. These names are mentioned in tablets found in Nineveh dating to the 7th century BC, however, the location of the town is unknown. Given how little is known for certain about the town, a transliteration of the Greek name is used in this translation.

2 Codex Sinaiticus: Genoeto to anoma to mega autou (ΓΕΝΟΙΤΟ ΤΟ ΟΝΟΜΑ ΤΟ ΜΕΓΑ ΑΥΤΟΥ). Translation: Genoeto the name the great his

As Genoeto (Γενοιτο) was used in the Septuagint as a translation for the word that the Masoretic Texts retains as Amen (אָמֵן), the name Amen is restored in this verse, and indicates that the Samaritans, or at least the author, viewed Amen as being the name of God. There are several other verses in the books not redacted by Simon the Zealot that show the Samaritans and Judahites were sun-worshipers before being conquered by the Assyrians and Babylonians.

In 1st Ezra, Pharaoh Necho II of Egypt claimed to have been sent by Lord the god to fight the Babylonians, however,

Necho II was a sun-worshiper, suggesting that the Sun was Lord the god in Judah at the time in the view of the author. King Josiah had banned the worship of the Sun, along with the moon, and Shamayim, in favor of Yahweh, and was subsequently killed by the Pharaoh, who then occupied Judah. Jeremiah, the prophet of Yahweh, who lived through this era claimed the Judahites were worshiping the wrong god, suggesting sun-worship was restored by Necho II, and Baruch later described the Sun and then stated it was the god of the Israelites in the Septuagint's book of Baruch.

3 Codex Sinaiticus: Achicar (ⲀⲭⲈⲓⲕⲀⲢ)

- Codex Vaticanus: Achiacharos (ⲀⲭⲓⲀⲭⲀⲢⲟⲥ)

- LXX 107: Achiachar (Ⲁⲭⲓⲁⲭⲁⲣ)

- Codex Corbeiensis (VL 150): Achicarus

- Codex Complutensis 1 (VL 109): Acicarus

- Codex Sangermanensis 4 (VL 7 : Achiacar

- Codex Bobbiensis (VL 135): Achicharus

- Codex Monacensis (VL 130): Achiar

The Codex Sinaiticus contains a curious version of Ahikar's name in this verse, which is otherwise the same as his name in the Codex Vaticanus. It appears to be a direct transliteration of the Aramaic version of the name Åhyqr (אחיקר), suggesting the Sinaiticus translation originally used direct translations of the Aramaic names, which were replaced with the common Greek translations at some point. In any event, the Sinaiticus version must have been translated directly from an Aramaic text in order to include a transliteration of the Aramaic version of the name, which supports the Sinaiticus version being older than the Vaticanus.

4 Codex Sinaiticus: Nabad (ⲚⲀⲂⲀⲆ)

- Codex Vaticanus: Nasbas (ⲚⲀⲤⲂⲀⲤ)

- LXX 71: Nabas (ⲚⲀⲂⲀⲤ)

- Sahidic manuscripts: Asbas (ⲀⲤⲂⲀⲤ)

- Codex Complutensis 1 (VL 190): Nabat

- Codex Regius (VL 148): Nabal

- Codex Monacensis (VL 130): Nadab

The name of the nephew is not standardized in the manuscripts. The nephew's name used in the surviving copies of the Words of Ahikar is Nadan, which is used in this translation as the copies of the Septuagint do not agree.

Tobit (Sinaiticus): Chapter 12

They completed the marriage, and Tobit called Tobiah his son and said, "Child, see that the man who went with you is paid, and you must give him a bonus."

Tobiah said to him, "Father, how much should I pay him? It won't hurt me to give him half of everything which I have brought back with me, as he has brought me back to you in safety, and saved my wife, and brought the silver to me, and also healed you. How much should I give him?"

Then he answered Tobiah, "It is justified, child, take half of all that you have brought," and he called him and said, "Take half of everything I have as your salary when you leave, and leave in peace."

Then he called them secretly and told them, "Praise God and thank him for the things which he has done to you in the sight of all that live. It is good to praise God, and exalt his name, and honorably to declare the works of God, and so don't be slow to praise him. It is good to keep private the secret of a king, but it is honorable to reveal the works of God. Do that which is good, and no evil will touch you. Prayer is good with fasting and charity and righteousness. A little with righteousness is better than much with unrighteousness. It is better to give charitably than to save up gold, for charity delivers from death, and will purge away all sin. Those who exercise charity and righteousness will be filled with life, but they who sin are enemies to their own life. Certainly, I told you the truth, and I will take nothing from you. For I said, 'It was good to keep private the secret of a king, but that it was honorable to reveal the works of God.' Now, therefore, when you prayed, and Sarah your daughter-in-law, I brought your prayers before the glorious Lord[1] and when you buried the dead, I was also with you. When you did not delay to rise and leave your dinner to go bury the dead, your good deed was not hidden from me, but I was with you. And so, God has sent me to heal you, and your daughter-in-law Sarah. I am Raphael, one of the seven holy messengers, which go in and out before the glorious Lord."

Then they were both troubled, and fell on their faces, for they were afraid. But he said to them, "Don't be afraid, for it will be well with you. Praise God, and do not ask any favor from me. By the will of our God I came, therefore praise him forever. All these days I appeared to you, but I did not eat or drink, as you were seeing a vision. Now, give praise on the Earth to the Lord and thank God. I go up to him that sent me. Write all the things which were happened to you."

When they rose, they no longer saw him. Then they praised and sang praise to God and praised his actions and his great name, as they'd witnessed the messenger of God.

Tobit (Sinaiticus): Chapter 12 Notes

1 Codex Sinaiticus: doxês cyriou (ΔΟΖΗCΚΥΡΙΟΥ). Translation: glorious Lord

- Codex Vaticanus: agiou (ΑΓΙΟΥ). Translation: saint

Tobit (Sinaiticus): Chapter 13

He continued, "Blessed is the god who lives for ages, and blessed in his kingdom. For he punishes and has mercy. He leads down to the grave and brings up again, and those he chastises and plagues, Shachar[1] leads from Hades, the lowest part of the Earth. He leads up from great loss, and none exist at all that can escape his hand. Tell of him to the nations you Israelites, for he has scattered us among them. Declare his greatness and extol him before all the living, for our Lord exists, and he is our God, and our father, and he is God of everything in their ages. He will have mercy on all of you where he scattered you among the nations."

"If you turn to him with your whole heart, and with your whole mind, and deal honestly before him, then will he return to you, and will not hide his face from you. Praise Lord Sydyk,[2] and praise the king of ages. In the land of my captivity, I praise him and declare his might and majesty to a sinful nation. You sinners, turn and do justice before him. Who can tell if he will accept you, and have mercy on you?"

"I will extol my God, and my mind will praise the king of the sky, and will rejoice in his greatness, and let the streets of Jerusalem sing of joyous love, and all of her temples sing, 'Hallelujah, praise God of Israel,' and bless and praise the holy name, in the ages and now! Once more, your tabernacle will have a temple built in joy, and celebrate you, and all taken captive will be greeted with affection by you, and all their discomfort and all their generations of ages."

"Bright light shines all the way to the edge of the earth. Nations from far off depend on you and all who live to the extremities of the Earth, and call you holy, and your gifts your hands hold, King of the sky.[3] Generation after generation is always going to give you joyful praise, and chose your name in all generations of ages."

"All accursed, love difficult words. Accursed is everyone who insults you, and pulls down your walls, and knocks down your towers, burns your temples, and blessed is everyone for the ages who fear you. At that time, they will go and rejoice greatly, those sons of the law. Everyone who collects and brings to, and praises the Lord of the ages, blesses and shows affection for the dead in your peace, and blesses all people you grieve and all you scourge, and you rejoice in that you will be able to see all your joy for the ages! My mind blesses the Lord, the Great King!"[4]

"Jerusalem will be rebuilt,[5] the city of his temple in all centuries is blessed. Those born from the remnants of the descendants will see your glory and praise the king of the sky. The streets of Jerusalem will be paved in sapphires and emeralds, and all the walls will be rebuilt of precious stones. The towers of Jerusalem will be rebuilt of gold, and the bastion from pure gold, and the streets of carbuncle, with beautiful gemstones from Sauvira.[6]

The streets of Jerusalem will sing joyously and cheerfully, and all her temples will sing, 'Hallelujah, blessed is the god of Israel, and blessed is the holy name for ages and now!'"

Tobit (Sinaiticus): Chapter 13 Notes

1 Codex Sinaiticus: eôs (ⲉⲱⲥ). Translation Eos (or dawn)

The Titan Eos, was the Greek goddess of the dawn, whose Canaanite equivalent was Shachar (שָׁחַר), who was referred to in the book of Isaiah as the father of the morning star, later translated by Jerome as Lucifer in the Latin Vulgate. Shachar was the god of the dawn in the ancient Ugaritic Texts, however, was still worshiped as later as the time of Isaiah, who lived at approximately the same time as Tobit, therefore, the Canaanite/early-Israelite name is restored as Tobit would not have been referencing a Greek Titan.

2 Codex Sinaiticus: ton cyrion tês dicaeosynês (ⲧⲟⲛ ⲕⲩⲣⲓⲟⲛⲧⲏⲥⲇⲓⲕⲁⲓⲟⲥⲩⲛⲏⲥ). Translation: the lord the justice

- LXX 249: ton theon tês dicaeosynês (ⲧⲟⲛ ⲑⲉⲟⲛ ⲧⲏⲥ ⲁⲓⲕⲁⲓⲟⲥⲩⲛⲏⲥ). Translation: the god the justice

- Codex Corbeiensis (VL 150): de dominus in iustitia. Translation: the lord in (or under, towards) Justinia

- Codex Bobbiensis (VL 135): de deum de iustitiam. Translation: the god the justice

The term 'the justice' (τῆσ Δικαιοσύνης) was used in the Septuagint for places where the Masoretic Texts retains the name Sydyk (צְדָק), the Canaanite god of justice. During the Roman era, the same name was applied to the Roman god Jupiter (Jove) as well as for the Roman spirit of Justice (Justitia) by Hebrew-speaking people, meaning the knowledge of Sydyk had not disappeared by the early Christian era.

3 Codex Sinaiticus: basili tou ouranou (ΒΑϹΙΛΕΙΤΟΥ ΟΥΡΑΝΟΥ). Translation: king the vaulted-sky (or Uranus)

• Codex Complutensis 1 (VL109): regem de caelum. Translation: king of the sky

• Codex Bobbiensis (VL 135): rex de caelum et terrae. Translation: king of the sky and land

The vaulted-sky (Ουρανου) of early Greek cosmology was based on, or very similar to, the Shamayim of the ancient Canaanite and Israelite religions, however, the term 'king' is more problematic, as the Aramaic word mlch (מלכא) is likely the source of the Septuagint's word Moloch, the name of one of the gods that Solomon set up an idol to in his temple.

The god in question was the Ammanite god mlk (מלך), whose name translates as king, however, the god's name is not pronounced in Hebrew as melech (מֶלֶךְ), meaning king, but preserves the Aramaic spelling as mwlch (מולך). This verse implies that Moloch was a title for Shamayim and Bethel, who certainly was a god being worshiped in the Temple in Jerusalem before King Josiah's reforms circa 625 BC, several decades after this book was apparently written.

4 Codex Sinaiticus: ton cyrion ton basilea ton megan (ΤΟΝ ΚΥΡΙΟΝ ΤΟΝ ΒΑCΙΛΕΑ ΤΟΝ ΜΕΓΑΝ). Translation: the lord the king the great

• Codex Vaticanus: ton theon ton basilea ton megan (ΤΟΝ ΘΕΟΝ ΤΟΝ ΒΑCΙΛΕΑ ΤΟΝ ΜΕΓΑΝ). Translation: the god the king the great

• LXX 58: ton theon ton basilea ton mega (τον Θεον τον μασιλεα τον μεγα). Translation: the god the king the great

Given the pronunciation of 'king' in Aramaic, this may have read 'the god Moloch the great,' however, that cannot be proven with the surviving texts, and so a more generalized translation is used.

5 As Tobit was reported to have died before King Cyaxares (Αχιαχαρος) of Media conquered Nineveh in 612 BC, and Jerusalem wasn't destroyed by the Neo-Babylonian Empire until 587 BC, Tobit could not have predicted the rebuilding of the city that had not been destroyed yet. Another Tobit may have made the prediction. On of the original Israelite leader who returned to Jerusalem in the book of Ezra was known as Tobit, however, he was later rejected as his lineage could not be proven. Followers of a priesthood of Tobit were later reported to be active in Moab during the Persian and Greek eras, which were most likely those who used the book of Tobit.

6 Codex Vaticanus: Souphir (ⲥⲟⲩⲫⲓⲣ)

• Codex Sinaiticus: Souphir (ⲥⲟⲩⲫⲉⲓⲣ)

• LXX 46: Ophir (Ο ⲫⲟⲓⲣ)

• LXX 583: Saphir (ⲥⲁⲫⲓⲣ)

• LXX 319: Souphêrô (ⲥⲟⲩⲫⲏⲣⲱ)

• LXX 107: Souphêrô (ⲥⲟⲩⲫⲏⲣ)

This quasi-mythical land of riches was also transliterated as Sophira (Σωφηρα) in other books of the Septuagint, and as Ofir (אוֹפִיר) in the Masoretic Texts.

The location of this civilization has been a matter of debate for ages. Given the list of items imported from Souphir/Sophira/Ôpîr, it was likely the ancient Pakistani Kingdom of Sauvira on the Indus River. Imported items include gold, silver, sandalwood, pearls, ivory, apes, and peacocks. Sandalwood trees are indigenous to South and Southeast Asia and have traditionally been considered sacred by the Hindus, Jainists, Buddhists, and Zoroastrians, as well as other Asian cultures. Peacocks are indigenous to South and Southeast Asia, as well as the Congo Rain-forest, however, Sandalwood trees are not found in the Congo Rain-forest. Apes were still living in South and Southeast Asia circa 1000 BC, along with most of Africa.

An alternate theory regarding the location of Sophira was that it was a trading port in Southern Arabia or Somalia, however, the ships of Solomon were said to take three years to travel between Edom and Souphir/Sophira/Ofir, which makes the location of Sauvira more likely. The Kingdom of Sauvira is listed in the ancient Late Vedic period and early Buddhist literature, as well as the Mahabharata, based around its capital of Rohri in the modern Pakistani state of Sindh.

This civilization is recorded as having existed from the Early Vedic period, before 1100 BC, meaning it would have existed in the time of Solomon. The capital of Sauvira was Aror, also called Roruka or Rorik in classical literature, which was one of the most important cities in South Asia in the 7th century BC, when this book was set. According to the Buddhist Bhallatiya Jataka, as well as Jain Story of Udayan and the town of Vitabhaya, the city of Aror was destroyed by a major sandstorm around 450 BC, following which the modern city of Rorhi (روبڑی / روهڙي) was founded around 10 kilometers away.

Tobit (Sinaiticus): Chapter 14

Here end the words of the statement of Tobit.

He died peacefully at 112 years old, and was buried honorably in Nineveh. He had been 62 years old when he became blind, and after becoming blind lived morally on charity donated to him, and yet put God first and praised the greatness of God.

When he was dying, he called Tobiah his son, and said, "Child, take your children, and move to Media, as I believe the declaration of God against Nineveh spoken by Nahum,[1] the everything that exists in Assur[2] and Nineveh, and as the prophet of Israel said, who was sent by God, 'All happened, and never did even one small word not happen, always it happened according to his time.' In Media exists salvation rather than in Assyria or in Babylon. Because I know and have faith whatever God said always takes place and happens, and not even a word fails from his message."

"Our brothers, the residents in the land of Israel, and everyone dispersed and taken captive from the land, and the goods, that exists in all the desolate land of Israel and the Samaria and Jerusalem are desolate and the temple of God is afflicted and set on fire for all time. Again God will have mercy on them, and God will return them to the land of Israel, and the temple will be rebuilt, not like the first at the dawn of time. It will be completed at the specified time, and with those returned from the captives, each and every one, who will rebuild Jerusalem and the Temple of God, and rebuild everything, as stated by the prophets of Israel."

"All the nations of the whole Earth, every one will turn and will genuinely fear God. Abandon all their idols, and those who cause to wander through cheating by lying about the planets, and praise the Lord for the ages in justice.

"All sons of Israel, those saved in all the days, who recall God in truth, and are collected and brought to Jerusalem and inhabit the land of Abraham in security, and safety for the ages. Rejoice and truly show affection for God, and abandon the errors and injustices of all kinds on the Earth."

"Now, child, I say to you, you worked for God in truth and you sang that which is acceptable in front of him. The children you made captives to bring justice and charity, and so they would remember God and praise his name for all time in truth and with their entire might."

"Now you, child, leave Nineveh and don't delay here. On the day you bury your mother with me, on that day, don't remain on this side of the border. Look around at all the injustice, and great deceit to gain through any means with no shame!"

"Remember, child, how Nadan treated Ahikar who raised him, not to live, but to be taken down into the earth? Yet God banished the dishonor against him and Ahikar came out into the light, and Nadan entered into the darkness for the ages for seeking to kill Ahikar. He gave charitably and escaped the snares of death which they had set for him, but Nadan fell into the snare and perished. Now, child, see what charity does, and what injustice brings?"

"My mind is leaving..."

They left him on the bed, and he died, and they buried him honorably.

They held an honorable feast in Ecbatana in Media, and invited the house of Raguel from Tobit's father.

He died at 117 years old in high esteem, however, saw and heard before he died, of the fall of Nineveh, and how she was captured and ruled by Media, and had been taken prisoner by King Cyaxares[3] of Media. He praised the God of everything, that he brought this on Nineveh and the Assyrians. He was cheerful that this happened to Nineveh before he died, and praised the Lord of ages and ages.

Tobit (Sinaiticus): Chapter 14 Notes

1 Codex Sinaiticus: Naoum (Nᴀoʏм)

• Codex Vaticanus: Iônas (ιωnᴀc)

Both Nahum and Jonah predicted the destruction of Nineveh. The Book of Nahum is internally dated sometime during and shortly after the Assyrian occupation of Egypt between 663 and 656 BC, and generally accepted as dating to that era, while Jonah is widely regarded as being fiction by historians.

The Book of Jonah is internally dated sometime during the Assyrian rule of Samaria, approximately 720 to 612 BC. If Jonah and Tobit were both real people, they would have been in Nineveh at the same time, and given the size of the Samaritan population in Nineveh, likely would have met.

2 Codex Sinaiticus: Athêr (ᴀɵнр)

• Codex Corbeiensis (VL 150): Assur

• Codex Monacensis (VL 130): Assyr

• Codex Bobbiensis (VL 135): Assyrios

Based on the contexts, it is clear that Assur, the capital of Assyria is intended, however, the Codex Sinaiticus' transliteration of the name appears to be based on the Persian version of the name: Athur (𐎰𐎠𐎢𐎼𐎠), suggesting the Aramaic translation was made in Persia or Media.

TOBIT (SINAITICUS): CHAPTER 14 NOTES

3 Codex Sinaiticus: Achiacharos (ΑΧΕΙΑΧΑΡΟC)

• Codex Vaticanus: Nabouchodonosor cae Asyêros (ΝΑΒΟΥΧΟΔΟΝΟCΟΡΚΑΙΑCΥΗΡΟC). Translation: Nabouchodonosor and Asyeros

• Codex Alexandrinus: Nabouchodonosor cae Asouchros (ΝΑΒΟΥΧΟΔΟΝΟCΟΡΚΑΙΑCΟΥΧΡΟC). Translation: Nabouchodonosor and Asouchros

• LXX 319: Nabouchodonosor cae Assyêros (Ν ܐܡܘܟܘܕܘܢܘܣܘܪ ܘܐ ܐܣܘܠܒܘܣ). Translation: Nabouchodonosor and Assyeros

• LXX 46: Nabouchodonosor cae Asoêros (Νܐܡܘܟܘܕܘܢܘܣܘܪ ܘܐ ܐܣܘܠܒܘܣ). Translation: Nabouchodonosor and Asoeros

• LXX 488: Nabouchodonosor cae Assoucros (Νܐܡܘܟܘܕܘܢܘܣܘܪ ܘܐ ܐܣܘܘܡܒܘܣ). Translation: Nabouchodonosor and Assoucros

This final line appears to be part of an anachronistic redaction. The Babylonian King Nabopolassar sacked Nineveh in 612 BC, along with Median and Persian allies. His son Nebuchadnezzar, who assumed the throne in 605 BC, finally conquered the remnants of the Assyrian forces in Syria at the Battle of Carchemish that same year, however, he did not destroy Nineveh. The name Asyêros (Ασυηρος) is generally accepted as a variant spelling of Ahasuerus (Ασουηρος), the Aramaic name of Xerxes, the Persian king who ruled between 486 and 465 BC.

The Codex Sinaiticus' does not mention either king, but gives credit to King Achiacharos (Αχιαχαρος) of Media, which is likely an attempt to transliterate the name Uvaxštra (⟨𒆠-𒌍𒋗𒁹𒍝⟩), which was also transliterated as Cyaxarês (Κυαξάρης) in Greek, from which his common English name is derived. Other ancient versions of his name include the Elamite Makiišturri (𒆠𒁹𒋗𒌷), Neo-Babylonian Úaksatar (𒌋𒐊), and the Phrygian Ksuwaksaros (ΚƧΟꟼΑႸƧΡΟƧ). Cyaxares was the Median king who fought alongside the Babylonian King Nabopolassar at the sack of Nineveh, following which Nineveh became part of his Median Empire. This seems clear proof that the Codex Sinaiticus version of Tobit is older, and more accurate.

Septuagint Manuscripts

The following is a list of the Septuagint manuscripts referenced in the notes for this book.

LXX ℵ (Codex Sinaiticus) is dated to the 4th century. Sections are currently located at the British Library (Add. 43725) in London, Leipzig University (Gr. 1) in Leipzig, the National Library of Russia (Gr. 2; Gr. 259; Gr. 843; Fonds. d. Ges. f. alte Lit., Oct 156) in St. Petersburg, and Saint Catherine's Monastery (Neus Slg. MΓ 1) on Mount Sinai.

LXX A (Codex Alexandrinus) is dated to the 5th century. It is currently located at the British Library (Royal 1 D. VIII) in London.

LXX B (Codex Vaticanus) is dated to the 4th century. It is currently located at the Vatican Library (Gr. 1209) in Vatican City.

LXX V (Codex Venetus) is dated to the 8th century. It is currently located at the Marciana Library (Gr. 1) in Venice.

LXX 44 is dated to the 15th century. It is currently located at the Stadtbibliothek (A 1) in Zittau.

LXX 46 is dated to the 15th century. It is currently located at the National Library of France (Coisl. Gr. 4) in Paris.

LXX 58 is dated to the 11th century. It is currently located at the Vatican Library (Regin. Gr. 10) in Vatican City.

LXX 64 is dated to the 10th century. It is currently located at the National Library of France (Gr. 2) in Paris.

LXX 71 is dated to the 13th century. It is currently located at the National Library of France (Coisl. Gr. 1) in Paris.

LXX 74 is dated to the 13th century. It is currently located at the Laurentian Library (S. Marco 700) in Florence.

LXX 76 is dated to the 13th century. It is currently located at National Library of France (Coisl. Gr. 4) in Paris.

LXX 98 is dated to the 13th century. It is currently located at the Royal Library (Σ-II-19) in El Escorial.

LXX 106 is dated to the 14th century. It is currently located at the Biblioteca Comunale Ariostea (187 I-III) in Ferrara.

LXX 107 is dated to 1334. It is currently located at the Biblioteca Comunale Ariostea (188 I) in Ferrara.

LXX 122 is dated to the 15th century. It is currently located at the Biblioteca Marciana (Gr. 6) in Venice.

LXX 126 is dated to the 1475. It is currently located at the State Historical Museum (Gr. 19) in Moscow.

LXX 130 is dated to the 12th or 13th centuries. It is currently located at the Austrian National Library (Theol. Gr. 23) in Vienna.

LXX 236 is dated to the 11th century. It is currently located at the Vatican Library (Vat. Gr. 331) in Vatican City.

LXX 248 is dated to the 13th century. It is currently located at the Vatican Library (Vat. Gr. 346) in Vatican City.

LXX 249 is dated to the 13th century. It is currently located at the Vatican Library (Pii. II Gr. 1) in Vatican City.

LXX 314 is dated to the 13th century. It is currently located at the National Library of Greece (44) in Athens.

LXX 318 is dated to the 10th or 11th centuries. It is currently located at the Vatopedi (598) on Mount Athos.

LXX 319 is dated to 1021. It is currently located at the Vatopedi (600) on Mount Athos.

SEPTUAGINT MANUSCRIPTS

LXX 392 is dated to the 10th century. It is currently located at the Abbey of Saint Mary of Grottaferrata (A. γ. I) in Grottaferrata.

LXX 402 is dated to the 14th century. It is currently located at the Patriarchal Library (Σάβα 105) in Jerusalem.

LXX 538 is dated to the 12th century. It is currently located at the National Library of France (Coisl. Gr. 191) in Paris.

LXX 542 is dated to the 9th century. It is currently located at the National Library of France (Gr. 10) in Paris.

LXX 583 is dated to the 14th century. It is currently located at the National Library of France (Gr. 1087) in Paris.

LXX 670 is dated to the 14th century. It is currently located at the Vatican Library (Vat. Gr. 335) in Vatican City.

Alternative Translations

The following is a list of alternative translations that were used for comparative analysis. Both the Peshitta and Coptic translations are believed to have been heavily based on the Septuagint, although do inherit relics of older Imperial Aramaic translations, or imports from the Hebrew translation.

The Peshitta is the Syriac translation of the Christian bible. The Old Testament was translated from older Aramaic and Hebrew sources during the late 2nd century AD.

The Sahidic manuscripts are translations of the Septuagint into Sahidic (also known as Thebaic), one of the six dialects of Coptic, the classical era form of the Egyptian language. Sahidic was the dominant form of Coptic used before the 11th century, and is believed to have originated in the region around Hermopolis, at the boundary between Upper and Lower Egypt. Translations of the Septuagint into Sahidic are known to have existed by the 4th century, however, early non-dialect specific translations are generally accepted as having been made as early as the 1st century AD, with some scholars suggesting the 1st century BC. The early non-dialect specific forms of Coptic are generally grouped with Sahidic, as Sahidic did not have a standardized spelling until the 6th century.

The Armenian bible was translated from the Septuagint in the 5th century, replacing the older Armenian bible that had been translated from Aramaic texts, however, includes some of the older names.

The Ge'ez manuscripts are Classical Ethiopic translations of various ancient Israel books that comprise the Christian bible, Jewish Tanakh, and Beta Israeli Orit. They were sources from texts in multiple languages, including Coptic, Greek, Aramaic, and Arabic.

The Vetus Latina are the old Latin translations of the Septuagint and other Israelite texts that predate Jerome's Latin Orthodox Bible in the 5th century. Some of the texts appear to have been translated directly from Aramaic or Hebrew source texts, however, most appear to have been translations from the Greek translations. The version of Tobit found in the Vetus Latina manuscripts is far closer to the Codex Sinaiticus' version of Esther than the more common versions found in Septuagint manuscripts, suggesting it was translated from an Aramaic source.

Codex Sangermanensis 4 (VL 7) is a copy of the book of Tobit which dates to 825. It is currently located at the National Library of France (Fonds lat. 11553), in Paris.

Codex Complutensis 1 (VL 109) is a copy of the book of Tobit which dates to 850. It is currently located at Complutense University Library, in Madrid.

The Codex Monacensis (VL 130) is a copy of the books of Tobit, Judith, and Esther which dates to 800. It is currently located at the Bavarian State Library (Clm 6239), in Munich.

The Codex Bobbiensis (VL 135) is a copy of the books of Tobit, Esther, and Maccabees which dates to 875. It is currently located at the Biblioteca Ambrosiana (E.26), in Milan.

The Codex Regius (VL 148) is a copy of the book of Tobit that dates to 850. It is currently located at the National Library of France (Fonds lat. 93), in Paris.

The Codex Corbeiensis (VL 150) is a copy of the book of Tobit which dates to 822. It is currently located at the National Library of France (Fonds#lat. 11505), in Paris.

Also Available

Also Available

- Octateuch: The Original Orit

Enoch and Metatron Series:
- Books of Enoch Collection

- Books of Enoch and Metatron Collection

- Books of Metatron Collection

- Secrets of Enoch

Other Translations:
- Apocalypses of Ezra

- Arabic Maccabees

- Life of Adam and Eve

- Memories of the New Kingdom

- Septuagint's Esther and the Vetus Latina Esther

- Septuagint's Ezekiel and the Ba'al Cycle

- Septuagint's Job and the Testament of Job

- Septuagint's Proverbs and the Wisdom of Amenemope

- The Amarna Letters

- Testaments of the Patriarchs Collection

- Tobit and Ahikar

- Ugaritic Texts: Ba'al Cycle

- Wisdom of Ahikar

www.ingramcontent.com/pod-product-compliance
Lightning Source LLC
Chambersburg PA
CBHW071145120626
46546CB00006B/2132

* 9 7 8 1 9 9 8 2 8 8 5 6 4 *